*How to Design and Deliver*
**Equal Opportunities Training**

**The Kogan Page Practical Trainer Series**

**Series Editor: Roger Buckley**

# PRACTICAL TRAINER SERIES

*KOGAN PAGE*

# *How to Design and Deliver*
# *Equal Opportunities Training*

## HELEN GARRETT AND JUDITH TAYLOR

KOGAN PAGE
Published in association with the
Institute of Training and Development

First published in 1993

Kogan Page Limited
120 Pentonville Road
London N1 9JN

**British Library Cataloguing in Publication Data**

A CIP record of this book is available from the British Library.

ISBN 0 7494 0848 0

Typeset by Saxon Graphics Ltd, Derby
Printed and bound in Great Britain by
Biddles Ltd, Guildford and King's Lynn

# Contents

# Acknowledgements

The authors would like to acknowledge the contribution of the following individuals and organizations to the production of this book:

    Judi Garstang, Training Adviser, Ministry of Defence
    Joan Orme, Equal Opportunities Studies Group, University of
       Southampton
    Members of the Greater London Council/Inner London Education
       Authority Training Units.

# Series Editor's Foreword

Organizations get things done when people do their jobs effectively. To make this happen they need to be well trained. A number of people are likely to be involved in this training by identifying the needs of the organization and of the individual, by selecting or designing appropriate training to meet those needs, by delivering it and assessing how effective it was. It is not only 'professional' or full-time trainers who are involved in this process; personnel managers, line managers, supervisors and job holders are all likely to have a part to play.

This series has been written for all those who get involved with training in some way or another, whether they are senior personnel managers trying to link the goals of the organization with training needs or job holders who have been given responsibility for training newcomers. Therefore, the series is essentially a practical one which focuses on specific aspects of the training function. This is not to say that the theoretical underpinnings of the practical aspects of training are unimportant. Anyone seriously interested in training is strongly encouraged to look beyond 'what to do' and 'how to do it' and to delve into the areas of why things are done in a particular way. The series has become so popular that it is intended to include additional volumes whenever a need is found for practical guidelines in some area of training.

The authors have been selected because they have considerable practical experience. All have shared, at some time, the same difficulties, frustrations and satisfactions of being involved in training and are now in a position to share with others some helpful and practical guidelines.

In this book, Helen Garrett and Judith Taylor provide guidelines for designing training in an area which often causes both trainers and trainees an element of discomfort, namely equal opportunities. Some trainers have described their experiences in presenting this kind of training as feeling as if they were 'walking on egg shells' or that every word that they used was being monitored by the 'thought police'. This should not be the approach to equal opportunities training and it is not the approach of this book. Equal opportunities is about removing barriers that prevent anyone from using their abilities to achieve their full potential. Obviously, this benefits the individual but it also makes good business sense for organizations to maximize the use of their human resources. While legislation relates, in the main, to gender, to race and disability, the concept of equal opportunity is wider and should apply to anyone who is prevented by unnecessary or unfair barriers from developing their potential.

This book is of value to all trainers and particularly those with little experience of introducing equal opportunities training to their organizations.

ROGER BUCKLEY

# Introduction

This new addition to the Kogan Page Practical Trainer series gives practical advice on a sensitive area of training which causes concern to many training personnel.

All employed people are entitled to certain legal rights, regardless of race, gender or disability, and the majority of large employers now have a statement of their commitment to the principle of equal opportunities. The implementation of such policies is more difficult. All too often employees think that equal opportunities is the responsibility of their employers alone, while employers believe that by adding a disclaimer to job advertisements they have done all that is necessary.

Perhaps more than any other, equal opportunities is a topic fraught with difficulties and pitfalls for the unwary. First of all, you are likely to encounter a range of negative feelings from apathy to downright hostility among those who need training. You may also encounter hostility from minority groups who feel that you are not the appropriate person to provide this training. Second, you really have to get it right first time. Handled badly, equal opportunities training can have the opposite effect to that which is intended, leaving trainees feeling guilty or resentful. The law is on the side of the trainer, and can be used to back up requirements for behavioural change, but a positive attitude can be encouraged by making training events interesting and enjoyable and giving trainees responsibility for their learning and their future behaviour.

Many training officers are aware of the need to do more on equal opportunities, but are uncertain of how to go about it, or lack the confidence to develop and deliver training events themselves. In this book we hope to show that, although you will undoubtedly require training yourself, you do not have to be a specialist to deliver equal opportunities training. Good sense, awareness of the issues and people's sensitivities, and a good knowledge of the law relating to equal opportunities and your organization's policies will enable you to carry out most of the training yourself.

This book aims to give you practical advice on how to plan, organize and run equal opportunities training programmes. Views expressed are the personal views of the authors, based on extensive experience, and should not be taken as a blueprint for success.

# 1  The Legal Background

 SUMMARY

- Using the main UK legislation, this chapter describes a number of the key concepts in equal opportunities:
  - Prejudice and discrimination
  - Direct and indirect discrimination
  - Victimization
  - Positive discrimination and positive action
  - Genuine occupational qualifications
  - Quotas and targets
  - Employers' and employees' responsibilities
  - Racial and sexual harassment.
- It then shows how these translate into policy and the consequent implications for your training.

Legislation to promote equality of opportunity is a relatively recent development in the UK. The earliest legislation, designed to deal with a specific problem, was the Disabled Persons Act 1944. As the date suggests, it was an attempt to respond to the employment problems likely to be faced by mentally and physically disabled military staff returning from the Second World War. Thirty years were to pass before any further equal opportunities legislation reached the statute books. The influence of the civil rights movement in the USA, including the Civil Rights Act 1964, which instituted equal rights on the basis of race, gender, nationality and religion, provided a spur to the development of similar movements in the UK, where legislation followed in the 1970s.

# Law and Policy

Underpinning the production of any equal opportunities policy is what can be described as anti-discriminatory legislation. In the UK this would include:

- The Disabled Persons (Employment) Act, 1944 (and 1958 and 1986)
- The Equal Pay Act, 1970 (and 1986)
- The Sex Discrimination Act, 1975
- The Race Relations Act, 1976.

More loosely related would be:

- The Rehabilitation of Offenders Act, 1974 – dealing with the employment rights of ex-offenders
- The Employment Act, 1991 – making discrimination on the grounds of trade union membership illegal.

For any policy to rely on the law alone, however, would leave many of them fairly thinly clothed. There is no law, for instance, against discriminating on the grounds of age, class, religion, sexuality or HIV infection; many of these however, are included in equal opportunities policies. Many of the practical outcomes of the legislation are not even mentioned in law. The Sex Discrimination Act, for example, does not make provision for workplace nurseries or flexible working schemes; these sorts of proposals have evolved through the implementation of policy, not law.

In broad terms the legislation could be described as laying down what people must *not do* whereas policies, while including these negative strictures, tend to move on to positive ways of fulfilling the spirit of the law in providing equal access, equal rights and equal opportunities.

### Why do I Need to Know about the Law?

Sometimes as a trainer you may feel that the answer to that is that when you have exhausted all your reasoning powers and it is nearing the end of a long hard day, you can do the equivalent of saying 'do it because I say so'. It can be consoling to have legal back-up! More seriously, if employees and indeed employers are to be held legally liable for their actions then it is only fair that they know this and are aware of the consequences. It is also useful for people to know that the policy is underpinned by law and did not drop from the clear blue sky. This does not mean, however, that you either need to be a legal expert yourself or that you will need to provide long and detailed briefings on the intricacies of the law to your colleagues. In the following paragraphs we have encapsulated the details which you really need to know; any further study will depend on your own interest and time.

We have used a question and answer format to cover the key concepts to make it easy for you to identify particular issues of interest to you but also to make it easy for you to extract relevant information for use on your own courses.

## Question 1. What is the Difference between Prejudice and Discrimination?

Prejudice is commonly defined as a personal belief that 'other people', their gender, culture, race, beliefs, are inferior to one's own. It is often based on generalized prejudgements rather than facts and maintained by a belief in stereotypes. These are frequently reinforced through education, parental or peer belief or the media, eg, young black men are good at sport; Asian people make good business people. (This is not to say that many educationalists and members of the media are not making strenuous efforts to counteract these influences.)

Discrimination is a systematic application of these beliefs (not necessarily consciously), particularly within organizations where means of access, systems, values and procedures have been developed by a predominant race, culture and gender reflecting their particular experience of the world. These organizations will naturally continue to perpetuate themselves by using systems and procedures designed by and for the majority. For example, organizations prior to the Acts regularly used criteria for promotion which disadvantaged women, such as length of continuous service or length of full-time service.

### The law

None of the legislation mentions personal prejudice explicitly but concentrates on the concept of unlawful discrimination. The title of the Equal Pay Act speaks for itself; it seeks to eliminate discrimination in an employment contract in the financial terms offered to each gender. The Sex Discrimination and Race Relations Acts prohibit discrimination in the terms of that contract, ie, in decisions on who to employ, what terms to offer them, who to train or promote. Both these Acts also prohibit discrimination in the provision of goods, services and education.

These laws are different from other employment legislation in that there is no qualifying period of employment or number of hours worked before a person can take a case alleging discrimination to an Industrial Tribunal. These laws apply to all employers, the only exemptions being employment in private households, employers with less than five employees (but only if they can demonstrate that they cannot extend their employment beyond a particular race or gender because of considerations of decency or privacy) and employees working wholly or mainly outside the UK. You may also wish to know that some discrimination is allowed in certain professions. For instance, the police can be required to be a particular height and there is a requirement to wear a particular uniform and use particular equipment. Prison officers can be required to be a particular height. Ministers of certain religions can be required to be a particular gender. Female mine-workers are restricted in the amount of time they can spend underground, whereas male workers are not.

### The policy and training implications

Most policies will require employees not to discriminate but are unlikely to mention personal prejudice. Some trainers in the early years of equal opportunities training did attempt to tackle prejudice through their training courses. The courses developed (often called 'race awareness courses') were designed to confront personal prejudice. The theory behind the training was that making people accept personal responsibility or feelings of guilt for the disadvantage suffered by members of ethnic minority communities would make them change their attitudes. Unsurprisingly, it was found in subsequent research that the effects of these often traumatic sessions wore off within about three months. There are a number of lessons in this.

First, that it is incredibly difficult to change attitudes and second, even if you can convince people to change, their return to an organization that has not changed means that they will soon realize they are powerless to make any difference and lose their incentive to try, although their personal behaviour may continue to be affected. More recently, trainers have focused more on the approach that you can train people to adopt acceptable behaviours but that you cannot do much about their beliefs.

In our experience, prejudice and stereotyping are the most intractable subjects to deal with on courses but, much as you may wish to stay on the relatively secure ground of behaviours, prejudice must be confronted if it arises. We have a particular memory of a white man on a course holding forth about the 'laziness of Afro-Caribbean workers'. When it was pointed out to him that he was insulting the Afro-Caribbean man sitting next to him he said, 'Oh I don't mean Jo, he's my mate'. We are sure that you can imagine the rest of the debate... 'Well, if he is an exception are there not others?'... and on and on.

To summarize: from our experience we recommend that your training focuses on an understanding of discriminatory practice and on the development of non-discriminatory behaviours. You may find that a change in behaviour produces a change in response which in turn may gradually influence a change in attitudes, but if you set out to achieve attitude change you may well be disappointed.

Although we have recommended an approach based on behaviour, you must be able to deal effectively with the occurrence of sexist or racist comments or other anti-equal opportunities opinions on your courses. It requires confidence in your own views, knowledge, patience, calmness and perseverence. Good luck!

## Question 2. What is the Difference between Direct and Indirect Discrimination?

Both are counted illegal under the Sex Discrimination and Race Relations Acts but they are two different concepts. People normally find direct discrimination easy enough to understand. It is defined in the legislation as being treated less favourably (not just differently) on the grounds of gender, marital status, colour, race, nationality or ethnic or national origins. Older people may well remember the pre-legislation days when signs like 'no blacks here' were legal or when jobs could be advertised for a particular gender – 'barman wanted'. The less favourable treatment can occur in employment, advertising, education and the provision of goods and services.

Indirect discrimination, a concept originating in American law, is more difficult for people to grasp because it is so much more subtle. It is defined as applying a condition or requirement to everyone (ie, being apparently fair) but the proportion of people from one gender or ethnic group who can comply with it is considerably smaller than the 'control' group. In addition, it must be shown that the condition or requirement is not justified and results in some detriment or disadvantage to the person from the gender or ethnic group who cannot comply with it. It is always useful to be able to illustrate the two points with some reference to Industrial Tribunal decisions.

### The law – direct discrimination

*Grieg versus Community Industry and Ahern (1979)*. Grieg was told she could not join a group of young people working on painting and decorating because she would be the only girl.

Found – direct discrimination.

*Khan versus Kent County Nurseries (1982)*. Khan was turned down for a job and received a letter saying, 'Regrettably I must decline your application since a young mum with three kiddies would be failing in her domestic duties to take up the opportunity that I offer'.

Found – direct discrimination.

### Indirect discrimination

*Malik versus British Home Stores.* The employer required employees to wear a uniform with an overall and skirt.

Found – the detriment to Muslim applicants for jobs amounted to indirect discrimination.

*Price versus the Civil Service Commission (1977).* The Civil Service required job applicants for executive officer posts to be between 17 and a half and 28 years old. Price was 35 years old.

Found – indirect discrimination as women tended to have children in their twenties and then rejoined the workforce. They were adversely affected by maximum age requirements.

### The policy and training implications

A requirement not to discriminate is often a cornerstone of any policy. As people can be largely unaware that the systems they use and their own actions are actually or potentially discriminatory, all staff will need to understand how discrimination operates. Training alone will not eradicate discrimination if systems and procedures remain unaltered but training should aim to give all staff the ability to critically evaluate what they do and how they do it. This is particularly important for gate-keeping staff who operate the barrier-points: recruitment, personal review or appraisal, promotion and access to training.

## Question 3. What does Victimization Mean?

It means treating somebody less favourably because they have either brought or intend to bring proceedings under the Sex Discrimination or Race Relations Acts or have given evidence in connection with proceedings brought by someone else.

### The law

There are a number of cases you can use to illustrate Industrial Tribunal findings in cases alleging victimization.

*Kipling versus Guardian Royal Exchange (1981).* Kipling, who had started grievance proceedings against their employer, was then subjected to harassment at work.

Found – victimization.

*Smith versus British Bata Shoe Co. Ltd.* Smith made an unsuccessful equal pay claim. She was then accused of gross negligence and demoted.

Found – victimization.

*The policy and training implications*
Unlawful discrimination by way of victimization needs to be included in training for managers.

## Question 4. What is the Difference between Positive Discrimination and Positive Action?

Positive discrimination, ie, discriminating in favour of previously disadvantaged groups is illegal. You cannot offer someone a job just because they are black or a woman (a common myth often presented as a reason to oppose equal opportunities). Positive action (affirmative action) is, however, legal and provision is made for it in the Sex Discrimination and Race Relations Acts.

*The law*
The legal scope for taking action to encourage equality of opportunity can be summarized under three headings:
1. Training
(a) Employers can mount special training programmes for people of a particular gender or race if, during the previous twelve months, there were no or a comparatively small number of people of that gender or race doing that type of work.

An example of such a scheme took place in Sheffield in 1991. City centre banks and building societies jointly employed 1,319 people, of whom 5 were from ethnic minorities. This represented 0.04 per cent of employees compared to 6 per cent of the total population of working age who were from ethnic minorities. The banks and societies funded 12 ethnic minority students on a 30-week banking course at a further education college. They were not able to offer a guarantee of a job after the course as this would have been positive discrimination; the students were, however better able to compete.

(b) Employers can also provide special training as above if the under-representation is in a particular level of work. An example of this would be the one-year Greater London Council accelerated management scheme for ethnic minority members of staff who were under-represented at management level. This combined studying for a Certificate in Management Studies with in-house courses, projects and a mentoring scheme. Again, in keeping with the law, no guarantee of promotion followed.

(c) Employers can provide special training or preferential access to ordinary training to people who have been excluded from regular full-time employment because they have been discharging domestic or family responsibilities. An example of this would be a retraining scheme for women returners to work.

2. Campaigning

Employers can campaign to encourage people of a particular gender or race to take up particular kinds of work if under-representation can be demonstrated as above.

3. Recruitment

If the same conditions apply, employers can positively encourage applications from under-represented groups through their advertising.

### The policy and training implications

In order to demonstrate under-representation you must have a monitoring scheme which will give you information about the gender and ethnic make-up of the employees in your organization. There is likely to be a training need for those designing and administering the scheme and a need for staff information sessions to explain the reasoning for the process. The provision in law for positive action is also the basis for positive action training programmes discussed in further detail in Chapter 5.

## Question 5. What is a Genuine Occupational Qualification (GOQ)?

A GOQ is a requirement for a job that it is held by someone of a particular gender or race. You can specify this in your advertisements provided that the job conforms to certain legal requirements.

### The law

The grounds on which you can specify race or gender for a job are detailed in the Sex Discrimination and Race Relations Acts as follows:

- Physiological – you can, for example, specify that you need a female model to model female clothes.
- Authenticity – you can ask for a male actor to play Hamlet.
- Decency or privacy – you can ask for a specific gender to preserve decency, eg, a female lavatory attendant.
- In single sex accommodation – if it is unreasonable to provide separate sleeping and sanitary facilities.
- Personal services or welfare – where the job involves a personal involvement in a group's welfare or educational services, eg, an Asian woman to work in an Asian women's refuge.
- Hospitals and prisons – if the establishment is single sex and it is reasonable to require someone of the same gender.
- Legal restrictions – if another UK law limits employment, eg, restrictions on women working in mines or where the job is in a country which restricts female employment, eg, Saudi Arabia.

### *The policy and training implications*

The implementation of your policy may include the identification of jobs where a GOQ could legitimately apply. It is important that people understand that this does not mean that favouritism or positive discrimination is operating. Some explanation of the meaning and rationale behind GOQs should be incorporated in your training courses. It will dispel resentment which could otherwise occur.

## Question 6. What is the Difference between a Quota and a Target?

The approach to equal opportunities in the USA included establishing a quota system for access to education. The quota system established a percentage of places in colleges for students of African-American, Asian, Native American or Hispanic origins. If their academic standards did not reach the required level that percentage was still admitted. If the number reaching the required standard far exceeded that percentage, entry was still restricted to that number. This approach would contravene the positive discrimination aspect of UK law.

### *The law*

The only instance in which a quota system has been introduced in UK law is in the provisions of the Disabled Persons Act. This requires employers of a workforce of more than 20 people to ensure that at least 3 per cent of that workforce are registered disabled people (green form holders). This is of limited value for two reasons. First, employers often apply for exemption from this requirement and are granted it. Second, there are in fact insufficient numbers of registered disabled people of working age for all employers to reach this quota (although some employers include for policy purposes anyone who defines themselves as having a disability whether registered or not). Very few companies have ever been subject to legal action for failure to comply and fines for those who have have been very low.

### *The policy and training implications*

Targeting as opposed to setting quotas for gender and race is perfectly legal, although not mentioned in law. Targeting involves not setting a maximum figure like a quota but setting a minimum figure to aim for and possibly exceed. Basically it means that as part of your implementation of a policy you set realistic targets for the changes you wish to achieve over a set period of time, ie, the number of women, people with disabilities or black or ethnic minorities you aim to have in particular jobs or at particular levels by a particular time chosen by your organization. This naturally leads into a process of action-planning to achieve this.

'Opportunity 2000' is a case in point, aiming to increase, by the year 2000, the number of women in senior posts in participating UK organizations, in line with targets set by those organizations.

It is self-evident that targets are unlikely to be met, let alone exceeded, by an organization sitting back and waiting until it happens by some process of osmosis. The organization will need to plan carefully how it is going to recruit and develop staff to reach these targets. This is likely to include a positive action programme with a significant training and development input.

## Question 7. What are the Various Responsibilities of Employers and Employees under the Legislation?

Employers are liable under the Sex Discrimination and Race Relations Acts for discriminatory acts conducted by themselves. They may also be liable for discriminatory acts conducted by their employees or agents, whether or not they are done with the employer's knowledge and approval.

Employers have a defence if they can show that they took such steps as were reasonably practicable to prevent employees from committing discriminatory acts. Employers are also acting unlawfully if they instruct an employee to carry out a discriminatory act.

Employees can also be personally liable for acts of discrimination. Any employee whose act has resulted in the employer being liable will be taken as also liable. It is a defence if employees can show that they acted in reliance on a statement made by the employer that the act was not discriminatory and that it was reasonable of them to believe that this was so.

### The law

There are a number of examples of Industrial Tribunals that can be used for illustration.

*Molloy versus Fine Fare Ltd (1983)*. A man applied for a clerical job but was told by an employee that the area manager wanted a woman.

Found – company guilty of sex discrimination.

*Dwyer versus Ciro Pearls Ltd (1982)*. Dwyer turned down for a job as a sales assistant and told in a letter that due to company policy the interviewer had favoured a woman.

Found – although there was no such policy the company was found liable for their interviewer's discrimination.

*Brown versus Newham Health Authority and another*. A black nurse was subjected to racial abuse by a payroll officer.

Found – both the Authority and the employee were found guilty of racial discrimination.

*Irving and another versus the Post Office (1987).* A postman wrote racially offensive words on a letter addressed to the Irvings.

Found – postman guilty of racial discrimination. The Post Office was not liable as the postman had acted outside the sphere of his employment.

### The policy and training implications

Policies will often state that responsibility for implementing equal opportunities lies with every employee. As ignorance or good intentions are no excuse, it is evident that people need training to ensure that they understand what their liabilities are. Your training must be very clear about what the employer and the law would consider a discriminatory act.

The employer may also take the view that the process of training staff in their legal duties satisfies the requirement laid upon them by law to take reasonable steps to prevent their employees from committing discriminatory acts. They may then argue that employees are solely responsible for their own actions. Whether or not this argument would succeed, it may give extra weight to your training, particularly if you wish to argue that any part of it should be made compulsory. You may well find management on your side!

## Question 8.  Is Racial or Sexual Harassment a Criminal Offence?

Although there has been some suggestion that France may move towards making sexual harassment at work a criminal offence, it is not so in the UK (unless it becomes grounds for an assault or rape charge).

### The law

Although harassment on racial or sexual grounds is not explicitly mentioned in either the Sex Discrimination or Race Relations Acts, it may amount to unlawful discrimination. If it creates intolerable working conditions which result in the person suffering some detriment they may be able to take a case under one or other of the Acts. If the harassment leads to the person suffering harassment being dismissed, being forced to resign or being deprived of promotion or training, they may be able to claim unfair (constructive) dismissal under the provisions of employment protection legislation. Most cases alleging harassment tend to reach tribunals through unfair dismissal claims but there are a couple of cases where claims arising from dismissal have been brought successfully under the Sex Discrimination or Race Relations Acts.

*Walsh versus William Rutter Management Holdings (1984).* Walsh was dismissed after pouring a glass of lager over the firm's accountant who had been persistently molesting her at a party.

Found – unlawful direct sex discrimination.

*Melkonian versus Zenith Engineering Ltd (1986)*. Melkonian resigned after suffering constant racial abuse and started work at another establishment for less money.

Found – direct racial discrimination resulting in financial detriment.

### The policy and training implications

Most policies eventually include, often as a separate document, a policy on dealing with racial and sexual harassment. It is often added to the disciplinary code as an act of gross misconduct. A number of training needs are likely to result from this:

- General staff training to set standards of 'professional' behaviour between colleagues and towards customers.
- Management training for managers to set and monitor standards and use disciplinary or grievance procedures to deal with breaches.
- Personnel or other specialist staff to advise or counsel victims of harassment and to investigate cases.
- Trade union training to enable them to support victims and represent members accused of harassment.

## Review

As you will appreciate, this is by no means an exhaustive résumé of UK legislation. There are some excellent summaries of the legislation available (detailed in the bibliography) and anyone who wishes to undertake a detailed study can always brave the full text. For most staff the legal background we have highlighted can be incorporated into general awareness/information sessions. An outline programme for such a session is included in the appendix.

For specialist staff we would, however, recommend detailed briefing sessions on the organization's legal obligations. If you are not a legal expert you may wish to bring in external experts to lead these sessions as they will need to be at greater depth than the outline in this chapter.

In addition to the areas we have covered, we have listed below the legislation which different groups of specialist staff will probably find useful to know:

- The main provisions of the Equal Pay Act, 1970, and those of the Equal Pay (Amendment) Regulations, 1983, ie, equal pay for the same or equivalent work (including pay for work of equal value)
  - for personnel staff and any staff working in job design or job evaluation.

- The retirement (pension) and maternity provisions of the Sex Discrimination and Equal Pay Acts
  – for personnel and payroll staff.
- The role of the Equal Opportunities Commission (EOC) and the Commission for Racial Equality (CRE), both of which have produced codes of practice on the promotion of equality of opportunity in employment. They also have a role in research, enforcement and assistance to individual complainants.
  – for personnel staff and senior management.
- The Employment Act, 1991, which prevents discrimination on the grounds of trade union membership (or non-membership)
  – for personnel staff and managers involved in recruitment.
- The Rehabilitation of Offenders Act, 1974, which lays down a scale of rehabilitation periods following conviction for a criminal offence, after which the conviction is spent and does not need to be revealed when applying for jobs. The only exceptions to this are:
  (a) where the job is exempt from the provisions of the Act; these broadly include jobs requiring professional qualifications, eg, doctors and barristers
  (b) jobs where the job holder would have access to vulnerable people, eg, children
  Full lists of the jobs in each category are included in the Act
  – for personnel staff and any other staff involved in recruiting or dismissing staff.
- Article 119 of the Treaty of Rome, continuing European Community directives and the 1991 European Commission Recommendation on the dignity of men and women
  – for personnel staff and senior management.

## Law into Policy

We have indicated the main areas of law which are translated into policy and which have implications for the training you will need to provide.

It may be that many employers take the minimalistic approach to an equal opportunities policy and concentrate on not contravening the law. Even in these circumstances, however, we have found that 'the law' is not a particularly easy concept to grasp. We have encountered managers who have said, 'I know that I must not discriminate but what does that mean I should or shouldn't do day-to-day?' This practical side must be addressed in your training, even if your policy goes no further than that. If it does go beyond the basics, then your next step is to become involved in the development of your policy and to start on your training plan.

# 2 Equal Opportunities and Your Organization

 SUMMARY

- Equal opportunities is important to ensure a fair society and effective organizations
- Training can help to overcome prejudice and develop skills
- Everybody needs training but some key staff have priority
- Responsibility for providing training should not rest solely with the trainer.

## Why is Equal Opportunities Important?

It is important because prejudice exists. Because it is unfair that people should be discriminated against for reasons of gender, ethnic group, religion, disability, age or sexual orientation. Because failure to make use of the skills and potential of all our citizens will mean a less skilled, representative, motivated workforce. Because it is good for business to have staff at all levels of seniority representative of the community as a whole. Because the law makes certain requirements of organizations and the people working in them, and the law must be obeyed.

All this means policies, procedures, and training.

## What Can Training Do?

Equal opportunities training helps organizations to implement their equal opportunities policies and familiarize people with new procedures.

It can help to overcome prejudice, ensure that legal requirements are met, develop skills and realize potential, and generally make the best use of human resources.

Most large organizations now include a statement to the effect that they are, or are working towards becoming, equal opportunities organizations. Many have policy statements, some of which are detailed enough to include policies on training and development. A selection of approaches by different organizations is given in the appendix.

## Who Needs Equal Opportunities Training?

The short answer is, 'everybody'. Ideally, all staff should be familiar with those parts of the legislation or company policy which refer to them and their work, and be aware of the importance of avoiding direct and indirect discrimination. The various Codes of Practice state that individual employees have a responsibility not to discriminate or knowingly aid their employers to do so.

If resources are limited, then give priority to senior people with the authority to bring about change, or consider selecting suitable individuals who might 'cascade' the awareness down (but bear in mind that they will require training and support if they are to have this role).

Training which deals directly with awareness and attitude change should be made available to all staff in a department or work group in order to prevent gains in awareness being adversely affected by peer-group pressure or routine workplace procedures which run counter to those advocated during the training. This kind of training also needs to be closely linked to developments in equal opportunities policies and procedures.

New employees need to be informed about equal opportunities during the induction programme, and some organizations ask them to sign a statement that they have read the policy and agree to abide by it.

In addition, there are people in certain key areas whose needs should be addressed. All who are involved in recruitment and selection of staff (or students, for those working in education) require training to ensure that applicants at each stage in the process are given fair and equitable treatment. This means not just the interviewers but all staff who are involved in any way in the recruitment and selection arrangements. Some organizations now insist that at least one and preferably all those who sit on interview panels should have had training in equal opportunities.

Other key areas are: job grading, allocation of duties, promotional procedures, appraisal, training, job transfer, merit rises or increments, treatment of grievances, discipline and dismissal. Key staff include receptionists, telephonists and other 'front-line' staff, section supervisors, first line and senior managers, board members, trade union officials, shop stewards or employee representatives, personnel and training staff.

What about training for under-represented minorities themselves? Positive discrimination is unlawful but positive or affirmative action is permitted when a group of employees have been under-represented over the past 12 months in particular work. Encouragement may then be given to them to take opportunities for doing that work and training provided to enable them to attain the skills needed for it. Such training might include management development for women, assertiveness and confidence-building for ethnic minorities, the opportunity to learn computing skills for older people re-entering employment after a career break, or re-training for a disabled member of staff unable to carry out his or her original job.

## Who is Responsible for it?

Responsibility for the management of staff development, and the implementation of equal opportunities policies, ultimately lies with the employer. Commitment at the most senior level is essential and should filter down through all levels of management. As far as equal opportunities training is concerned, any form of discrimination is a barrier to the effective working of the organization and it is everybody's responsibility to see that it is removed.

It is important that a senior member of staff is given responsibility for the overall coordination of equal opportunities policy and the training plan and there should be regular consultation between managers, individuals and those directly responsible for providing the training. It may be useful to assemble a small team of colleagues from a variety of sections and levels who are committed and interested in the subject. They can help with the planning of both strategy and tactics, and may be very influential in disseminating information and increasing awareness throughout the organization.

All managers have a responsibility for the staff working for them. The existence of a training unit, or an equal opportunities committee, should not allow individual managers to opt out of all responsibility for training in this area. Individuals should also be encouraged to take responsibility for their own training needs. The precise role of the training officer will vary from one organization to another, being affected by such things as culture, size, attitudes of managers, as well as the training officer's own knowledge, perceptions, skills and interests.

More specifically, the following should be taken into consideration:

- organizational structure
  - where is the focus for change?
- organizational plan
  - preparing people for change: reactive or proactive?
- degree of autonomy
  - management structure: to whom do you report?
  - committee structure: do you have a committee? Does it have any power?
  - financial control: how much do you have?
  - do you have policy making and/or executive responsibilities?
- support staff
  - what skills and experience do they have?
- other resources
  - training room? Training material? Expertise within the organization?
- history
  - the 'we've always done it this way' factor.

## The Role of the Trainer

These considerations will also affect the kinds of activities which the trainer undertakes. Every trainer will undertake some of the following activities – and most will undertake all. You should ensure that you have assessed your own training needs and taken appropriate action before undertaking equal opportunities training. A useful checklist is given in Chapter 3, page 37.)

- direct training
- designing learning opportunities
- training administration
- advising management
- advising individuals

However, the amount of time spent on each of these will vary according to the considerations mentioned above. Two possible models are given in Figure 2.1.

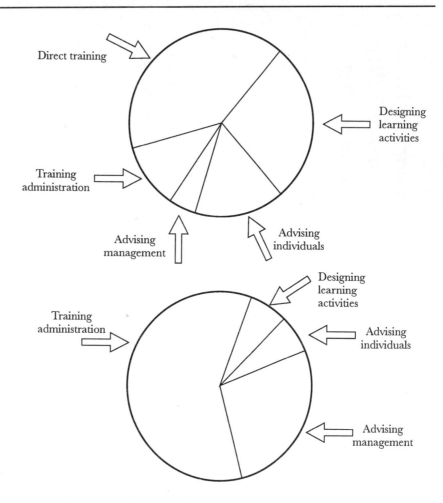

**Figure 2.1** *Two possible trainer models*
(Diagram based on *The Trainer's Programme Unit 2: What do trainers do?'*, Local Government Training Board, 1984)

If you are uncertain about your role, look at your job description to see which items relate to which activity, and also check with the person to whom you report to see what she or he thinks your priorities and key tasks should be.

You may also like to consider your preferred style of work. Do you prefer telling, selling, sharing or facilitating? You may find that you need to adapt your approach according to the situation and the people whom you are training. Figure 2.2 suggests a 'sliding scale' approach.

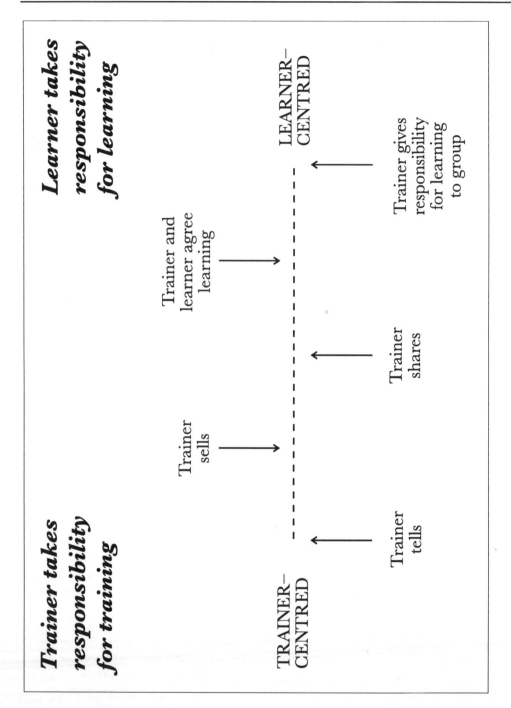

**Figure 2.2** *Preferred training approaches*

(Adapted from R Tannenbaum and W Schmidt, *How to Choose a Leadership Pattern*, Harvard Business Review, March–April, 1958).

Telling may be more appropriate for some key staff who need to know the behaviour which is expected of them; more senior staff may react better when given the responsibility to decide what and how they will learn. There are no hard and fast rules; your preferred style, the culture of the organization and the knowledge and attitude baseline of its staff, and the learners themselves, will all need to be taken into account.

# 3  Identifying Training Needs

                    SUMMARY

- This chapter gives guidance through the practical steps involved in identifying equal opportunities training needs:
  - Assessing your own training needs
  - Steps to action; from the policy to the analysis of who and what needs to change
  - Working out your programme: a competency-based model
  - Identifying positive action training needs
- It includes case studies, sample questionnaires and checklists to help with the process.

It is not the purpose of this chapter to describe in detail training needs analysis methodologies as this has been done many times before. Our intention is to provide some practical guidelines through the maze of equal opportunities training needs and some tools you can adapt to your own use. If you are like us and can remember your early days as a trainer, you probably recall using a number of techniques: repertory grids, semi-structured interviews, observation, critical incident techniques and a plethora of questionnaires.

These are all valid methods of assessing needs but which of them are the most effective in identifying equal opportunities training needs? We hope to give you some guidance later in the chapter, but we will first look at some of the features which make equal opportunities training needs analysis slightly different from, say, the training needs arising from new technology.

## What is Different about Equal Opportunities Training Needs?

1. The introduction of a policy of equal opportunities has implications for the work of every single person in your organization. You will be faced with a huge range of needs from common 'core' ones based on broad policy requirements, eg, no one shall discriminate, to highly specialized ones, eg, assessing positive action training needs for women into management schemes.

---

### TIP 1

Do not start everywhere at once. It is vital that you go through a process to establish priorities; we will suggest one process later in the chapter using a prioritizing grid (see Figure 3. 2).

---

2. You may have very few (or even no) 'experts' guiding the policy or able to help you with defining how different, for example, the requirements of a manager's job within an equal opportunities context are from what went before.

---

### TIP 2

In the absence of in-house resources, you will probably be expected to be the expert. Even if you intend to involve external consultants to assist in the training you will:

– not be a good role-model for staff commitment if you do not play a key role in the implementation yourself
– always know more about your own company/organization and its policies and culture than any external person can hope to do.

Your first question in this whole process will therefore be, 'What are *my* needs for training, development and support?' A self-assessment form to help you to look at this is given in Checklist 1.

---

3. You may find that you are expected to start providing training when the policy is no more than a broad statement of intent before procedural change has occurred; the needs can often then feel disconcertingly nebulous.

---

**TIP 3**

We strongly recommend that you are personally involved in the policy development process. Involvement in the evolution of the policy will enable you to effectively link it with training. You will find it very difficult to train without an understanding of procedural change and associated issues.

---

4. Equal opportunities brings in not only skills and knowledge but that vexed question of 'attitude' and/or personal beliefs and prejudices. How on earth do you assess that? It is an area where people are rather less than likely to be frank about their beliefs, particularly if you want them to fill in a questionnaire about them.

---

**TIP 4**

Concentrate on required behaviours rather than attitudes when assessing training needs; it is far easier to observe and far less threatening to your interviewees or observees.

---

5. As we believe that the way any trainer approaches the assessment of training needs has an impact on the commitment of trainees to the subsequent training or development, we feel it is important to get people to see that it is relevant to them and their job. We will quote the man in one organization who asked, 'How do I serve a hamburger in a non-sexist way?'

---

**TIP 5**

If practicable, choose methods of training needs evaluation which require personal contact. Sample interviews, either individually or in groups, allowing an exchange of information and the opportunity to raise queries are probably no more time-consuming than either attempting to analyse a mass of questionnaires or having to start again because nothing came back to you. As it is our belief that managers should play a major part in training needs analysis, this should not be as time-consuming for you as it might sound. Questionnaires are really most useful for establishing facts (who, how many, etc.).

---

6. It involves change across the organization similar in many ways to the experience of those companies like British Telecom who have

introduced Total Quality Management. We are frequently told that people do not like change and will resist it.

---

TIP 6

At least at the level of knowledge about the underlying reasons for the policy, you need to consider the training needs of all staff. To ensure that changes are not seen as being designed from 'above' and dumped on them via you as a management mouthpiece, this should be at an early stage in the evolution of the policy. Finally, do not expect overnight miracles; you definitely will not get them.

---

## Before you Start

We have in the previous paragraphs suggested that there are two preliminaries to embarking on a training needs survey – preparing yourself and preparing everyone else.

### Yourself

- Ensure that you have assessed your own training needs. Do you have the appropriate skills, knowledge and understanding of your own attitudes?

Checklist 1 is a useful way of giving some thought to your own state of readiness. You can note down what you need to do to rectify any gaps in your own skills, knowledge and attitudes. The actions may include training, meetings – internal or external – setting up a support network and the study of appropriate material.

A list of useful external contacts and literature is included in the appendix. Remember, you don't need to be perfect to make a start, just confident about the basics.

---

CHECKLIST 1 – SELF-ASSESSMENT

1. Do you understand the relevant legislation and codes of practice?
2. Do you know the organization's equal opportunities policy and its relationship to other personnel policies?
3. Do you have the confidence and skills to identify and deal with prejudice, stereotyping, racism, sexism and other anti-equal opportunities comments or actions?
4. Do you have access to the policy development process?

5. Do you have sufficient knowledge of your organization's structure and culture?
6. Do you have the training skills to design and/or run courses incorporating equal opportunities?
7. Have you got support inside the organization to deal with hostility, negativity or frustration?
8. Do you have a network of other people in equal opportunities from whom you can get ideas?
9. Do you have senior management support?
10. Are you personally committed to the implementation of equal opportunities?

**Everyone Else**

Provide information in more than written form to *all* staff about the policy as early in its formative stages as possible. The information should increase understanding and hopefully promote commitment. This is one time that you can proceed without conducting a needs survey; assume that nobody knows very much about the background, let alone the terminology or objectives of the policy and you will not be far wrong!

CASE HISTORY

A local authority publicized an equal opportunities policy statement to all the staff; it used expressions such as 'direct and indirect discrimination', talked about access targets, monitoring and evaluation. Following distribution of the policy document, the authority, having correctly identified recruitment as a key barrier to equal opportunities, substantially altered its procedure and made it mandatory for any interviewers to attend a course on selection interviewing. The course was designed (without a training needs survey) on the assumption that everyone had a high level of understanding about equal opportunities as they had all received a copy of the policy. It soon became clear that not only did people fail to understand the terminology in the policy, they had no idea why they were being asked to do things differently, were frequently resentful, felt de-skilled, felt that they were not qualified to question interviewees about attitudes to equal opportunities and couldn't relate the equal opportunities in recruitment with its apparent absence in the rest of their working lives.

*Result:* In many areas nothing much changed; procedural change does not by itself produce action.

It might be appropriate to say at this point, although it is not strictly part of identifying training needs, that a quiz used at this time as part of

**TO ALL STAFF**

*Lunchtime seminar on the introduction of equal opportunities.*

Do you need to attend the seminar on equal opportunities? Well, try completing this questionnaire. The answers are given below, but if you want to know why they are right or wrong, come along and find out.

|    |                                                                                                                    | TRUE | FALSE |
|----|--------------------------------------------------------------------------------------------------------------------|------|-------|
| 1. | Every employer has to have 3 per cent of their employees registered disabled.                                      | ☐ | ☐ |
| 2. | Positive action means discriminating against men in favour of black people and women.                             | ☐ | ☐ |
| 3. | Equal opportunities means I have to call a 'manhole' a 'personhole'.                                               | ☐ | ☐ |
| 4. | A Frenchman was refused a job in a Chinese restaurant; this is unlawful discrimination.                            | ☐ | ☐ |
| 5. | School children these days have to sing 'Baa baa green sheep'.                                                     | ☐ | ☐ |
| 6. | The law allows you to run women-only courses.                                                                       | ☐ | ☐ |
| 7. | Eighty-five per cent of the 12,000 registered blind and partially-sighted people employed in the UK have some vision. | ☐ | ☐ |
| 8. | You can ask women about their childcare arrangements at interview as long as you ask men as well.                 | ☐ | ☐ |
| 9. | Continuous length of service is a fair way of deciding on promotions.                                              | ☐ | ☐ |
| 10.| You have to work for an employer for two years full-time before you can take a case alleging discrimination to an Industrial Tribunal. | ☐ | ☐ |

SCORE

0 – 9   See you at the Seminar

10   See you at the Seminar – you are running it!

ANSWERS

[1] F;   [2] F;   [3] F;   [4] F;   [5] F;   [6] T;   [7] T;   [8] F;   [9] F;   [10] F.

the invitation to an information session about the policy can be entertaining and provoke curiosity. An example is given in Figure 3. 1.

**Figure 3. 1** *An example of an invitation to an information session*

## Putting the Policy into Practice

You should by now feel confident, with the workforce at least informed if not yet actively involved! Time to move on.

As your progress in developing the training will be loosely linked to the policy and its implementation, we have outlined below the key points of a typical equal opportunities policy to use as an example in the remainder of this chapter.

Most policies include a statement about:

- the changes in procedures needed to remove barriers to access to the organization.
- the need for people to behave in a non-discriminatory or anti-discriminatory way.
- the need to change the way in which people progress within the organization.
- the introduction of conditions of service designed to improve opportunities.
- how the service (or facility or product) will meet the needs of diverse customers.
- the systems and mechanisms to be introduced to facilitate implementation of these changes.

### Steps to Action

*Step 1. What needs to change?*
You will need to identify for each point in the policy:

- What needs to change (procedures/activities)
- Who needs to change (knowledge/behaviour).

If you are lucky, the first point will have been or be in the process of being decided and implemented by the people responsible for the conduct of the policy. If not, you may find Checklist 2 offers some guidance. It is based on an analysis of each of the points in the sample policy, to which you will be able to add your own.

## CHECKLIST 2 – PROCEDURES AND ACTIVITIES

| *Policy Statements* | *Procedures/Activities* |
|---|---|
| Access | 1. Job evaluation |
| | 2. Job design |
| | 3. Job description |
| | 4. Person specifications |
| | 5. Recruitment |
| | 6. Selection (interviewing) |
| Behaviour | 7. Grievance |
| | 8. Discipline |
| | 9. Management/supervision [who sets standards] |
| Progression | 10. Personal review/appraisal |
| | 11. Succession plans |
| | 12. Setting promotion criteria |
| | 13. Training/development |
| Conditions of service | 14. Pay (equal value) |
| | 15. Working conditions |
| | 16. Leave |
| | 17. Job-share |
| | 18. Child care/maternity leave |
| Service/product | 19. Product design |
| | 20. Customer relations |
| | 21. Marketing (research and sales) |
| | 22. 'Professional' activities (these need to be defined by your organization) |
| Implementation | 23. Monitoring |
| | 24. Training/development |
| | 25. Target setting |

### Step 2. What needs to change first?

Having established what needs to change, you have to ask the question, 'What happens first?' Each of the procedural and behavioural changes in the policy is likely to produce a training need, so you need to establish priorities. Again, these might have been determined for you by the people implementing the policy but if you are involved in the process it is a good idea to use two criteria to make some judgements:

- level and immediacy of impact – can systems be changed quickly, will they produce immediate measurable change and involve a relatively small number of people?
- a critical path approach, ie, what needs to happen before something else can?

If you find it helpful to use a mechanism to work out priorities, you may find that completing the prioritizing grid in Figure 3. 2 gives you a framework for discussions.

**Figure 3. 2** *Prioritizing grid*

In Checklist 2, Procedures and Activities, we have listed 25 possible changes linked to the policy. The prioritizing grid is a method of applying each of the two criteria above to each item by a process of paired comparisons.

For demonstration purposes I have used only 10 of the 25.

| | | | | | | | | |
|---|---|---|---|---|---|---|---|---|
| 1.2. | | | | | | | | |
| 1.3. | 2.3. | | | | | | | |
| 1.4. | 2.4. | 3.4. | | | | | | |
| 1.5. | 2.5. | 3.5. | 4.5. | | | | | |
| 1.6. | 2.6. | 3.6. | 4.6. | 5.6. | | | | |
| 1.7. | 2.7. | 3.7. | 4.7. | 5.7. | 6.7. | | | |
| 1.8. | 2.8. | 3.8. | 4.8. | 5.8. | 6.8. | 7.8. | | |
| 1.9. | 2.9. | 3.9. | 4.9. | 5.9. | 6.9. | 7.9. | 8.9. | |
| 1.10. | 2.10 | 3.10. | 4.10. | 5.10 | 6.10. | 7.10. | 8.10. | 9.10. |

( You can continue in this sequence up to any number. )

On the first line of the grid you will see 1 and 2 (job evaluation and job design). You first compare items 1 and 2 according to the two criteria. Whichever one rates higher, you circle. On line two compare 1 with 3 and 2 with 3. When you have finished, count up the number of times each was circled. Re-copy your list of 1–25 beginning with the item that was circled most often. If you have a tie, the number which was circled first counts more highly.

### Step 3. Who needs to change?

You have now been through stages:

1. What needs to change?
2. What needs to change first?

You are now ready for:

3. Who needs to change?

This is once again related to the policy and the changes in procedures, activities and behaviours it has outlined. You may, in a small organization, be able to immediately identify who the key people are from your own knowledge, from using organizational charts or from existing job descriptions. If you cannot, a quick paper survey will do. All you need to do is to transfer your list of key items (the 25 in our sample) onto a form and ask each section/divisional or departmental head to identify the people involved in any of these activities. It should be completed in minutes.

*Step 4. Working out your programme*
You have by now got a framework for your training; all you need to decide next is what to put in it!

**Figure 3. 3** *A model programme*

---

### A MODEL PROGRAMME

A common progression in implementation is:
1. Training in support of procedural change (recruitment, selection, discipline)
2. Training to promote work practices internally and in service terms which are free of discrimination: to provide a work climate which supports and promotes equality of treatment and opportunity (fair management, assertion, harassment, customer care, job design to promote the employment of people with disabilities)
3. Training to redress the effects of past discrimination and to positively promote opportunities for members of previously discriminated-against groups to develop the skills to progress into areas and positions where there is under-representation (access and positive action programmes, eg, women into management training).

NOTE: In effect little or no training-needs analysis is undertaken; the training is entirely policy-driven and everyone is assumed to need the same training.

---

The 'model programme' outlines a process followed by most public and private sector organizations and is based on a logical progression. You need monitoring systems set up, for example, before you can identify areas of under-representation. You will probably have identified a similar pattern if you have gone through the steps we have suggested. You still need to know, however, what to put in your programmes and you will find your training much more successful if it is related to existing levels of skill, knowledge and attitudes in your organization.

You now come to the training-needs analysis proper.

## Training Needs Analysis

Armed with your knowledge of the new procedures emerging from the policy and knowing who needs training in what, you can begin the process of narrowing down the needs. A problem-based approach to training-needs analysis is not really appropriate to equal opportunities, so we will be recommending a competency-based approach.

Just a reminder at this point that you will not of course be performing this process in a vacuum. You can also use analysis and evaluation of the content of your existing courses to inform your decisions about new training needs, eg, if you already run an interviewing course, what difference to its content or methodology does the policy make?

If you need to start from scratch to develop a competency model, there are three reasons why you will need to talk to the person(s) responsible for each of the functions:

- To develop a competency model based on actual practice
- To enable them to feel that they are contributing to, rather than being subject to, the training
- To continue the process of spreading information about the changes being brought about by the policy.

In discrete and specialized areas, such as recruitment, you will easily identify who to talk to. For more general areas such as 'management', you will need to decide on a sample. There we would recommend holding group rather than individual interviews. Time-saving is one factor but the idea-generating power of a group is an even more important one.

### The Competency-based Model

*First stage*
*Develop a model* for desirable or required competences, ie, establish the knowledge, skills and behaviours required in that job to operate effectively within an equal opportunities context. The competency statements should aim to be as precise and specific as possible.

*Method*
Interview a competent practitioner and, if you have time, observe them in operation – then you can check out whether what is said is actually what is done.

**Figure 3. 4** *Example – Assessment of the recruitment function*

**RECRUITMENT**

| | |
|---|---|
| **Who to talk to** | Personnel Officer/Head of Recruitment |
| **Documentation** | Current practice notes |
| | EO procedural guidelines |
| | Job descriptions/person specifications |
| **Sample questions** | 1. What does a recruiter do? |
| | 2. What will a recruiter have to do differently under the policy? |
| | 3. What makes an effective recruiter? |
| **Process** | Develop a series of statements: |

- 'a good recruiter needs to know'
- 'a good recruiter needs to do'
- 'a good recruiter needs to behave'

RESULTS

You will end up with statements like:

- 'A good recruiter needs to know which publications attract applications from black and ethnic minority applicants'.
- 'A good recruiter needs to know the provisions of the anti-discrimination laws'.

If you then ask yourself 'how' they will do and know and behave in these required ways you will be well on your way to determining the content of your courses or other learning mechanisms. This is the subject of another chapter.

You may decide that this is where you stop in the process and that everyone you have identified earlier as having any part to play in any of the activities, procedures or behavioural requirements defined in the policy is invited (or ordered!) to attend a series of standard courses in the particular topics. This is certainly an option, as we have already mentioned, and one followed by a number of organizations. If, however, you have the time and you think your training should start by recognizing that people in the organization are all at different starting points, that your training should be tailored to meet differing needs and that you would prefer participants and their managers to be involved in the process of planning and later in evaluation, then you will probably want to continue to stage two of the process.

*Second stage*
Establish the present level of performance and specify need.

*Method*
By discussion between the manager/supervisor and staff either individually or in homogeneous groups. Your role at this stage is to provide the manager with a checklist based on the agreed competences for them to use as an assessment tool to identify gaps (Checklist 3 provides an example of an outline checklist completed for a member of staff). If you wish to be even more sophisticated, you can also provide a series of rating factors based on:

● Importance in the work
● Present level of competence
● Extent of training need

for the manager to use (Checklist 4 provides an outline example completed for a member of staff, with ratings shown). NB. If you prefer this approach, with minor adaptations the forms can be used for self-assessment by staff.

---

### CHECKLIST 3 – COMPETENCES FOR THE RECRUITMENT FUNCTION

### RECRUITMENT

Staff member............................................................................................

Section/Division/Department ..................................................................

| *Competences* | *Met/Not Met* | *Comments* | *Training Need y/n* |
|---|---|---|---|
| KNOWLEDGE | | | |
| (1) Knows provisions of anti-discrimination laws | not met | not familiar with terms 'direct' and 'indirect' discrimination | y |
| (2) ... | | | |
| SKILLS | | | |
| (1) Is an effective listener as demonstrated by comprehensive interview notes | met | | n |
| (2) ... | | | |

BEHAVIOUR
(1) Does not ask               not met               Thinks it               y
potentially discriminatory                           shows concern
questions at interview                               to ask about child-care
                                                     arrangements

(2) . . .

---

## CHECKLIST 4 – RATING STAFF MEMBERS' COMPETENCES IN THE RECRUITMENT FUNCTION

### RECRUITMENT

Staff member.................................................................................................................

Section/Division/Department.........................................................................................

| Competences | Importance N/L/M/H | Present Competence 1 to 8 | Training Need N MI MO MA |
|---|---|---|---|
| KNOWLEDGE | | | |
| (1) Knows provisions of anti-discrimination laws | H | 3 | MA |
| (2) . . . | | | |
| SKILLS | | | |
| (1) Is an effective listener | H | 7 | N |
| (2) . . . | | | |
| BEHAVIOUR | | | |
| (1) Does not ask potentially discriminatory questions | H | 1 | MA |
| (2) . . . | | | |

*Key:*
*Importance* in present job is measured as being none, low, medium or high (N, L, M, H)
*Present level* of competence is measured along a range from poor to excellent:
1 / 2 / 3 / 4 / 5 / 6 / 7 / 8
poor    fair    good    excellent

*Training need* comes from looking at the first two columns and is measured as none, minor, moderate or major (N, MI, MO, MA)

If you have decided to embark on the second stage you need to keep in mind that:

- managers may need some briefing before they undertake the assessments
- it should be clear that it is only to be used for training needs purposes and should not form part of someone's performance review
- you need to decide whether you keep the information and use it yourself to determine the level of your courses and to target priority course participants or whether the manager retains it and uses it to arrange course attendance and to evaluate change while you receive only a summary of major needs from each area.

### Continuing the Process

This process can continue for all the changes in employment and service areas identified in the policy but additional methods of assessing need will become evident as you begin your programme:

- As courses start to run you can collect information from course participants
- Job descriptions may well be revised to identify specific responsibilities for equal opportunities in each job performance, which can be assessed through personal review or appraisal schemes
- Cases of discrimination or harassment may be highlighted through revised grievance or disciplinary procedures identifying specific training needs
- Monitoring information can be used to identify areas for concentration on positive action training.

## Identifying Positive Action Training Needs

As you will know from Chapter 1, the Race Relations Act and the Sex Discrimination Act both make provision for what we have called 'positive action training'. The training we have referred to in the main body of the chapter is primarily concerned with supporting actions to stop discrimination and remove barriers to entry and progression. This in itself will not, however, promote equality of opportunity. Groups who have traditionally not had the opportunity to develop skills or gain experience in particular fields will continue to be disadvantaged unless positive measures are taken to train and develop them.

It makes sense to tackle the training in the order we have done as positive action programmes cannot hope to be more than tokenistic if traditional barriers, perceptions and procedures are still in place. You will also need to know areas and levels of under-representation from monitoring figures before you can start to plan positive action training. You are not likely to be in a position to do this, in our view, until the policy is at least into its second year of implementation.

## The Process

In the assessment of positive action training you will be looking at two main areas:

● access to the organization
● progression through the organization.

*Access*
To assess the needs in this area you will need to know:

● monitoring information about the current make-up of the organization
● monitoring information about applicants for jobs.

You can then ask two questions: first, are the groups identified in your policy not applying for jobs in any significant numbers and, second, are they applying but not being appointed?

If the groups are not applying, your response is unlikely to include training. Your organization will need to consider using the other positive action provisions, ie, positive encouragement including outreach work and positive advertising. The Metropolitan Police have taken this approach in attempting to increase black and ethnic minority representation in the police force.

*Note:* In our experience, as an organization gets a reputation for being a 'real' equal opportunities employer, the number of applications from women, black and ethnic minority people and people with disabilities rises significantly.

If the groups are applying but being rejected, you will need to check a number of things:

● Are the job descriptions and person specifications discriminatory?
● Is the interview panel operating in a prejudiced way?
● Are the applicants less skilled and/or less experienced than the successful applicants?

If your training within the organization has been implemented effectively then the first and second questions should no longer apply, and you can look more closely at the third. If this holds true, your organization may decide to become involved in pre-entry access training to offer opportunities to these groups to develop the skills and experience needed to increase their chances of applying successfully for jobs.

This sort of training requires the commitment of considerable resources. Most organizations who have embarked on such schemes have done so in conjunction with higher or further education institutions, with the organization providing the work experience element of the scheme. Some successful examples of schemes are included in Chapter 5.

### CASE STUDY

The London Fire Brigade found that women were applying to become firefighters but failing the pre-entry test. The test included a large number of questions of a technical or mechanical nature about heights, weights, volume and velocity. The different nature of women's secondary education and experience left them at a disadvantage compared to men. The Fire Brigade established a college-based six-week pre-entry course for women. It was designed to rectify this relative lack of skill. The women took the test at the end of the course with a significant increase in the success rate.

### *Progression upwards*

If the monitoring information about existing staff in the organization shows that the groups are well represented only up to particular levels or only represented in certain areas, then you are likely to have identified another potential training need. If you establish, as is common, that women are well represented at more junior levels but not in supervisory and management positions, you will need to establish the reason. The first thing to check is that there are no discriminatory barriers still in operation, eg, continuous service as a requirement for promotion. If not, then you need to establish whether there is a training or development need. You can do this by a two-stage process:

- Look at the requirements for the next level job – job descriptions, person specifications and/or competency standards
- Interview a sample of women in the jobs or grades below. The interview should seek to assess whether the women possess:
    - the required level of skill
    - the required level of knowledge
    - the required type/length of experience
    - the confidence to apply.

If there is a gap in the skills or knowledge, this indicates a training need and you can design courses or use external educational provision to fill this. If the gap is in experience, your training needs to be designed to link with opportunities for job secondments, job rotation or mentoring schemes. If the gap is in confidence, you may wish to run some women-only career development/confidence building workshops and/or set up support networks.

*Progression sideways*

If the under-representation occurs not at levels but in particular areas, eg, technical sections, then you need to establish whether any of the under-represented groups currently in the organization wish to move into these areas. An open session describing opportunities in these areas will usually establish level of interest.

The assessment of training needs is usually more straightforward, as the reason for under-representation is frequently a lack of professional or technical qualifications. If your organization intends to offer opportunities for staff to gain these, you will need to do two things:

1. Be prepared to sponsor long term educational courses for the staff
2. Set up trainee posts in the new area of work so that people studying gain appropriate experience.

Not many organizations are able or willing to go so far, as it is a costly operation. If, however, there is a national shortage of the skills required there is some sense, in more than equal opportunities terms, in 'growing your own'.

## The Final Stage

If you have followed the processes of training assessment in your organization you should by now, apart from being thoroughly exhausted, be in a position to set up a range of training and development activities designed to produce change throughout the organization. Your next question is what and how. This is the subject of the next chapter.

# 4

# Approaches to Equal Opportunities Training

    SUMMARY

Once your organization is committed to equal opportunities training, and you have undertaken a training needs analysis, you need to consider the best approach for your organization. This chapter looks at:

- The training plan should make clear what the priorities are:
  - What must, should and could be done
- The pros and cons of the following approaches are discussed:
  - Separation or integration of equal opportunities training?
  - Focus on behaviour or attitudes?
  - Who should carry out the training: the in-house trainer or an external consultant?
  - On-the-job or off-the-job?

## What Must, Should and Could be Done

Most organizations have limited resources to spend on training and on equal opportunities (writing in 1992, in the midst of recession, this is truer than ever). It is likely that the training officer will have to argue for resources against other departments. It is therefore important to decide what must be done, what should be done, and what could be done if resources permit.

## What Must be Done

All staff need to know about the law in so far as it affects them, and in particular the different forms discrimination can take and why they should be avoided. Selection and interviewing skills are a crucial area which must be covered. We explained in Chapter 1 that employers may be liable under the Sex Discrimination and Race Relations Acts for discriminatory acts conducted by their employees or agents. Ignorance or good intentions are no excuse and it is therefore essential for training to be provided so that employees (who can also be held personally liable for acts of discrimination) understand what their liabilities are.

## What Should be Done

Staff should have a good knowledge of their organization's equal opportunities policy and understand the concept of fairness which underlies this. This will help them to understand the need for monitoring, and for positive action and encouragement to those who have been discriminated against to compete equally in the workplace. If a scheme for monitoring staff is to take place, it is important to set up regular advisory meetings to tell people why it is necessary and allay any fears they may have. Without this, the response will be low and the exercise meaningless.

General awareness raising should be a theme running throughout any training provided in equal opportunities; whether or not it should be addressed directly is discussed later in this chapter.

## What Could be Done

What could take place if resources permit would be seminars on the wider implications of discrimination, interpersonal and supervisory skills (including guidance for managers on handling accusations or incidents of discrimination), positive action and positive encouragement programmes, and perhaps opportunities to be forward-looking and innovative in terms of equal opportunities development.

# Separation or Integration of Equal Opportunities Training?

A question which often arises is whether separate equal opportunities training courses should be set up, or whether the training should be incorporated into more general courses. On the whole we recommend the integrated approach: not only is the training then likely to be more palatable, but equal opportunities is seen as an integral part of the management function. There may be occasions when it needs to be treated separately: familiarization with new organizational policies, for example monitoring; training departmental representatives or trainers; briefing senior managers and personnel staff.

There may be problems with the integrated approach if you rely on other people to carry out this aspect of the training who are inexperienced or unwilling, and you may need to monitor that it takes place. You also run the risk of it being seen as an 'add-on' extra unless it is carefully integrated ('Time for the equal opportunities session now'). Integration, however, protects it from short-term policy changes, and makes it more acceptable –

> trainers who were not closely identified with equal opportunities programmes could have a useful impact if they were confident in introducing equal opportunities issues on the management programme for which they were responsible (Commission for Racial Equality, 1989).

## Training Material

All trainers need to ensure that any training material they use is free from bias. Language is particularly important, and elderly handouts may need to be brought up to date! A title like 'Chairman' carries the implication that it applies only to men. Is it really necessary to say woman doctor or male nurse? Don't make the mistake of always referring to bosses as 'he' and secretaries as 'she'. The English language is limited by not having a neuter pronoun, but it is perfectly possible to use gender-free language without much difficulty. There are several guides to avoiding discriminatory language; the example given below comes from the National Union of Journalists.

| Instead of | Try |
|---|---|
| business man | business manager, executive, boss |
| cameraman | photographer, camera operator |
| newsman | journalist or reporter |
| fireman/men | fire fighter, fire crew |
| dustman | refuse collector |
| foreman | supervisor |
| policeman/men | police, police officer |
| man or mankind | humanity, human race, humans |

| | |
|---|---|
| manpower | workers, workforce |
| manning | staffing, jobs |
| manmade | synthetic, artificial |
| housewife | often means shopper, consumer, the cook |
| mothers | often means parents |
| girls (of over 18) | women |

Videos, slides and other illustrative materials are difficult and expensive to alter, but should not be used if there is any chance that they might be seen as prejudiced against any particular group. All too often people in senior positions are portrayed as white males, while secretaries are female; customers and clients are white while service staff are black; and people with disabilities are never seen leading normal lives, but only as a problem which the video seeks to address. And virtually everybody is under 35!

All material should be screened to make sure that it does not:

– perpetuate stereotypes
– demean or trivialize either sex, or any race or minority group
– show examples of discriminatory language or actions.

## Should the Focus be on Behaviour or Attitudes?

The Training, Enterprise and Education Directorate's (formerly Manpower Services Commission) 'Glossary of Training Terms' defines training as a 'planned process to modify attitude, knowledge, and skill through learning experience to achieve effective performance in an activity or range of activities'. As far as employers are concerned, 'activity' means work-related activity; what an employee thinks, feels or says outside work is only of interest to the employer if it impinges on the individual's work.

Many trainers believe that attitude change cannot be addressed directly, but can only be an indirect result of increased knowledge and improved skills. They prefer to concentrate on ensuring that the staff for whom they are responsible behave in accordance with the law and their organization's policy, arguing that an individual's attitudes are the concern of that individual alone and only become the concern of the employer if negative attitudes affect behaviour.

However, others believe that behaviour is bound to be affected by attitudes, and that it is therefore necessary to address these directly, usually through awareness training. These trainers argue that the behavioural approach is too 'soft' and conservative and that people and their prejudices should be challenged.

Attitude change, whether overt or implied, is, however, a particularly important feature of equal opportunities training, and there continues to be a great deal of discussion about it. Those supporting its open inclusion argue that without attitude change there can be no real progress; those against it argue that people's attitudes are their own private affair and the organization can only stipulate behavioural requirements.

## Awareness Training

Racism Awareness Training (RAT) was developed in the United States in the 1970s, and became popular in this country in the 1980s. It is used with all-white groups to help them to 'own' the problem of racism and become aware of the history of their negative and often oppressive relationships with black people. All-black groups are helped to understand what causes racism and to develop a black consciousness to help them with personal development. Although initially embraced enthusiastically, there is now resistance to the idea that racism is a white problem affecting all white people. Even if this were the case, RAT runs the danger of increasing guilt and, potentially, resentment. Its positive benefits, too, have been found to be short-lived.

Cultural awareness training can be helpful for managers and others who supervise the work of a multicultural workforce by introducing them to aspects of culture, dress, language and belief which may influence the way the work is carried out and the managers' responses.

Sexism awareness training may include assertiveness and general self-development courses for women, and can be helpful in increasing effectiveness at work and political awareness. Male awareness training is similar to RAT, but helps men to recognize that stereotypical male/female characteristics are often the products of conditioning, not innate.

Equal opportunities trainers themselves should consider attending courses like these, as it is difficult to recognize and try to overcome prejudices in other people without first becoming fully aware of your own.

# Who Should Carry Out the Training?

There are no absolute answers to this question; much will depend upon the organization, in particular its size and the resources available to it. What is clear, however, is that any 'generalist' trainer must have thorough training before tackling equal opportunities. Trainers should also carefully examine their own beliefs and attitudes, and scrutinize the training unit and the courses it provides to make sure that its practices are not discriminatory.

**In-house Trainers**

As a minimum, all in-house trainers need to:

● be familiar with the legislation, codes of practice, and organizational policy (and keep up to date with changes);
● understand their implications for personnel procedures;
● be able to identify and handle effectively prejudice and incidents of discrimination;
● have support from elsewhere in the organization.

Support is very important as trainers may face hostility or frustration from members of staff who feel that the pace of change is too fast, or too slow.

**The Use of External Consultants**

Equal opportunities is something which affects all staff, and you may need to use a mixture of outside 'experts' and in-house staff. The consultants could be used to train the trainers, and perhaps for any particularly sensitive piece of work such as racial harassment, or training for very senior managers. Some large organizations have a network of departmental or sectional representatives, who are the first point of contact for anyone with an equal opportunities-related problem. After training they should be competent to run informal workshops within their departments. An organization which has developed this approach is the University of Southampton (see the appendix).

In-house people have the advantage of knowing the organization and being familiar with its personnel, as well as its policies and procedures. However, there are times when familiarity can be a disadvantage, and the in-house equal opportunities trainer may face one of two problems: 'Oh, it's only so and so with another bee in her bonnet – equal opportunities this time!', or you may be too closely linked to senior management and its policies – a problem if they are unpopular. An outside consultant will be, and will be seen to be, more objective, will by his or her very presence make it clear that yours is not the only organization going down this particular road and, if they specialize in this area, are likely to be more up to date and better able to answer difficult questions than you, as a generalist trainer, can be. For all these reasons, a good consultant may have greater credibility. However, if you decide to bring in outside consultants, allow time for them to gain some familiarity with your organization.

You should take the following considerations into account when selecting outside consultants:

● Who else has used them? Was it a success? Is the other organization similar to your own?

- What experience have the consultants had? Can they offer a range of approaches? Do they have a particular expertise in one area?
- Do they have a clear policy on equal opportunities issues?
- Will they be able to challenge constructively negative attitudes which may be expressed to them?
- Will they be willing to spend time with your organization in order to find out about its culture, policies, staff, etc?
- What will they charge? Make sure that you know whether the fee is inclusive or exclusive of travel and other expenses, preparation time, etc.

Here is a checklist of some of the advantages and disadvantages of using in-house, and external, trainers:

## CHECKLIST

### In-house Trainers

| *Advantages* | *Disadvantages* |
|---|---|
| Familiarity of trainer with organization and staff | Familiarity of staff with trainer! |
| Involvement with development of policy and strategies | Close links with senior management may be unpopular |
| Availability for on-going training outside training room | |
| Cost effective | |

*Use for* regular briefings, updatings, familiarization with organizational policy and legal requirements, most interviewing training, 'quality service' training, awareness training for junior and middle level staff.

### External Consultants

| *Advantages* | *Disadvantages* |
|---|---|
| Objectivity | Expensive |
| Specialist expertise | Unfamiliar with organization |
| May be more acceptable to senior managers | No input into policy |
| May be more acceptable in sensitive areas | Cost considerations usually mean use limited to course provision |
| | Limited ability to follow through training in workplace |

*Use for* senior staff, introduction of new concepts (eg, to get your equal opportunities training programme started), sensitive areas such as racism awareness, sexual and racial harassment.

**Trainer Requirements**

The Commission for Racial Equality has highlighted six needs which all trainers working in equal opportunities have:

- **Support** from senior management as well as access to key decision-makers
- **Networking** with others working in this area. This includes specialist bodies such as the Commission for Racial Equality (CRE) and the Equal Opportunities Commission (EOC) as well as trainers in other organizations
- **Information** – a regular flow of information concerning training material and new developments is vital
- **Input to policies** on wider equal opportunities issues is important for trainers who should not be confined to training issues
- **Status** – all trainers are concerned about their status and the importance given to training. Low status and low importance are particularly detrimental to equal opportunities work
- **Training** of the trainers should not be overlooked.

The CRE also identified important skills or attributes which all equal opportunities trainers need:

- interpersonal skills, including the ability to cope constructively with confrontation; the ability to motivate and persuade people at all levels of the organization (and we would add skills to counsel and reassure)
- good communication and negotiation skills
- a commitment to equal opportunities
- knowledge of organizational development methods.

# On-the-job or off-the-job?

The pros and cons of on-the-job and off-the-job training have been documented many times. Generally speaking, on-the-job training is suitable for simple tasks and refresher training, or as a follow-up to off-the-job training. Our feeling is that most equal opportunities training should be done off-the-job, although you may wish to evaluate the effectiveness of the training by observing staff at work, for example on reception desks, or during interviews.

You should also consider whether it is likely to be more effective to send someone on an external course. People often gain from finding out how things are done in other organizations, as well as being less inhibited about admitting to prejudices, or even more liberal beliefs, than they would be in front of their work mates. External courses may also be more appropriate for senior managers for similar reasons. Senior staff may well come away from an external course either with a feeling of pride – 'We're doing better than Bloggs', or of competition – 'Bloggs seem to take equal opportunities seriously, and they are doing rather better than us'.

# 5 Planning a Training Programme

 SUMMARY

- This chapter takes you through the stages in setting up your training:
  - Understanding your organization
  - Preparing your training plan, the range and resources
  - Tactics for implementing your plan
  - Types of positive action programmes
- An example of a first-year plan and the training and resources needed are provided as a guide.

It is always nice to start with a plan:

- It focuses the organization's mind on progress
- You have something to measure action against
- You can build logically and systematically on existing learning
- You will gain a sense of achievement and pro-activity
- People know where they are going and why.

On the other hand, of course, it can become a bit like the proverbial oil-tanker, impossible to stop or turn! It is not very helpful to tell people that you can only slot their need in five years hence. Seriously though, you will need a plan or framework for your training, otherwise you will be in danger of hopping from issue to issue, missing out key areas and generally feeling in a permanent state of crisis. You should, however, be prepared to renegotiate priorities. The training plan should be continually monitored (preferably formally each month) so that it evolves alongside the policy. If you find, however, that you need to change it constantly you probably started off with the wrong plan!

In our view the plan should include:

- The training topic(s)
- Who the training is for
- When it will be delivered
- How it will be done

and for those who need to know:

- What it will cost.

You may also like to consider whether the plan should be formally adopted by your organization so that all staff are aware of its status and importance.

## Before the Plan

You need to undertake quite a lot of preparatory work before you can produce a detailed plan. Most importantly, you need to know three things:

1. What your organization is like
2. What the range of the training activity will be
3. What resources will be allocated to it.

We have outlined below some of the questions you need to ask yourself and others before you start drawing up your plan.

### 1. Your Organization

*What is the size and structure?*
The size of your organization will determine the scale of your training plan and whether you will be able to treat the organization as a whole or will need to break it down into more manageable units; it will also determine how long your programme will take. It will also help you to determine percentage or numerical targets for training take-up each year. The structure will determine your approach to implementing the plan: do you need the support of top management in a hierarchical structure or are managers in decentralized departments fairly autonomous? Defining who has the power to make things happen will immeasurably aid success. As equal opportunities develops, your analysis of the structure will extend to using monitoring information to determine

where there are blockages or under-representation. This is a basis for planning positive action programmes.

### What functions does it perform?

Do departments' functions vary greatly; will all managers need the same training; will some areas or people be more responsive to equal opportunities than others? Where will your training have the most impact on the main functions of the organization?

### What is the organizational philosophy?

Thinking about the values your organization has and the way it thinks is useful, in that it will help you to predict its reaction to various situations. If your organization is 'task-orientated', how can you demonstrate that your training will help it to be more effective? If it is concerned with the effective functioning of the people in it, how will you show that equal opportunities will have a beneficial effect on working relationships?

### What is the working climate like?

The working climate affects the way that people interact with each other. Organizations exist somewhere along a continuum from open and cooperative where learning is encouraged, to competitive, concerned with survival and not conducive to learning. The climate will have some effect on the way your training will be accepted.

### How does your organization cope with change?

Organizations are always changing, whether under external or internal pressure like new staffing or new technologies. Equal opportunities combines both pressures. Initially it can be seen as being imposed from outside or above, but if successful it will result in staffing and procedural changes which will build an internal momentum for change. Successful change depends largely on the ability of the organization to be flexible in its response. The ability and attitudes of managers are influential factors in effecting this, so management training should form an important element of your training.

### What is the attitude towards, and expectation of, training?

Your organization's response to and commitment to your training will be influenced by past experience, as will that of the staff. It will obviously be more difficult to introduce equal opportunities training if little training has occurred before or if it is seen as the exclusive reserve of the young or of 'high-flyers'. The type of training will also be influenced by expectations: people who have been encouraged to be self-developers will need to be convinced of the value of attending a course (and indeed do they have to?) Manual staff used to learning on-the-job may not take kindly to the back-to-school feeling of sitting all day in a course room.

## 2. The Range of Your Training Activity

*How much should I try to do?*

It will not be possible to do everything at once! Equal opportunities training and development should be viewed as an evolving process which will take years rather than months. Be realistic about how many things you can tackle and ensure that others understand this. As we have suggested, one way of doing this is to involve others in the development of your plan and publicizing it widely.

*Should I concentrate on short-term or long-term needs?*

It is tempting to concentrate on short-term provision meeting those needs which are more quickly and easily observed. You will be most effective if your training is linked to the long-term goals of the organization. We would say, however, that there is no harm in running a few events in sympathetic areas that show immediate returns, just to make your training visible!

*Are there any priority areas I should concentrate on?*

You need to decide whether you are going to start with information training for all staff; start with senior management; start with particular systems or procedures; or start in a particular part of the organization. These decisions need to be made in conjunction with the people responsible for the implementation of the policy but it is a good idea to have thought about this in advance.

*What effects will the status and function have on my training proposals?*

Is your status and that of the training function sufficiently high to be accepted as qualified to run the programme? Do you need a mentor at a more senior level? Are there parts of the programme you do not feel qualified to run? (Unless you are superman/superwoman there undoubtedly will be. ) If you follow a systematic planning process, your status and visibility are both likely to rise. If your organization is new to equal opportunities it is also quite possible that you will be hailed as an expert, so be prepared for your own rapid learning curve.

## 3. What Resources will You have Available?

*What are the resources?*

*People:* How many and who will you need to work on the programme? Are they external or internal? Do they need training? What contacts do you have? What internal expertise is available?

*Materials:* Do you have accommodation and equipment to run courses in-house or will you need to go outside? Do you need time to research and write your own material?

*Money:* You need to have costed your programme before you present it; is additional money available or will you have to switch resources? Main costs are likely to be for external trainers, course fees and publicity.

*Time:* How much do you have to contribute to the equal opportunities programme? How much time do you have within which to deliver the programme? Is it realistic? You also need to remember the time constraints on people attending courses when you plan how your programme should be delivered.

### Are there any constraints on the use of resources?

Inevitably there are constraints on the availability of resources, in particular, money. Hopefully you will be able to negotiate a reasonable budget if you can demonstrate through your plan how it will be spent. Do not, however, spend a lot of time developing a highly sophisticated plan until you have some broad indication of the likely level of your resources, otherwise you will be wasting time and inviting frustration.

### Who controls the resources?

You need to establish who controls the money as your programme is likely to be costly in time and money. You also need to consider who controls the time of the people who will be attending your programme. Will they allow their staff to be absent from work to attend equal opportunities programmes? How will you persuade them that it is worthwhile?

### How much priority should be given to resources for equal opportunities?

Initially the investment needs to be high to give some sort of momentum to the exercise. You need to ensure, however, that resentment is not created by a perceived switch of resources from existing training to equal opportunities. Positive action programmes tend to be very resource-intensive, so should not be embarked upon until the conditions have been established to guarantee a better than average chance of success.

### How many resources will I need?

This depends on a number of factors: priorities, timescale, size of the programme and an analysis of the consequent costs. You should include accommodation costs, equipment, consultant charges, printing, travel and refreshment, books and material. If you are intending to conduct much of the work yourself, you can have a basic programme for as little as £1,000, but you are likely to have more impact with a minimum of £5,000. The maximum is up to you and the generosity of your employer!

## Preparing your Plan

By going through the pre-planning exercise you should have a framework for conducting your training needs analysis, described in Chapter 3. In turn, the training needs analysis will inform future planning. You need to bear in mind, however, that you are likely to already have a training programme running and that you will not be able to halt all of it while you prepare an equal opportunities programme. In our experience, progress is best made by following up introductory equal opportunities seminars with a gradual integration of equal opportunities into existing courses. This can be linked to the staged introduction of new courses related to specific areas of change arising from policy implementation. Once these are well established you can then concentrate on researching and developing positive action programmes. During the development of an integrated programme you do need to keep it under review, using evaluation information. Regular discussions with those implementing the policy and with management and trade unions will help inform your future planning. Regular up-dates to staff via a newssheet or a regular column in a house journal are well worth the investment of time.

We are now going to take you through the stages in preparing your plan.

## Case Study – The Organization

This example of a training plan is based on a public sector organization with 2,000 staff in professional, technical, administrative, clerical and manual grades divided between 13 departments. The organization has a full-time training manager, one training officer and an assistant. A second training officer has recently been appointed with some responsibility for equal opportunities training. There is an equal opportunities adviser in post and a working group responsible to senior management for the implementation of the policy. The organization has an established training programme of in-house courses for junior/middle-range staff, mostly taught by internal tutors. It also has a one-year development scheme for graduate managers and a five-day senior management course run by external consultants. Fifteen people are sponsored each year to take professional and managerial qualifications. There is a budget of £50,000 to pay for course fees, external consultants, materials and publicity. The plan below was developed six months after the policy had been formally adopted and work on procedures had already begun. The existing training programme continued, although at a reduced level.

## The Training Plan

The priorities underlying the first year plan were:

1. To gain commitment at a senior level
2. To ensure that all staff understood the background to equal opportunities and why it was being introduced. The priority groups to be those in direct contact with the public
3. To start to remove barriers to access (recruitment and selection)
4. To ensure key staff had specialist knowledge of employment issues (maternity rights, part-time and flexible working; equal pay)
5. To develop a common core module for managers on their responsibilities under the policy, including the training and development of their staff
6. To train other members of staff to assist in briefings and training
7. To begin to evaluate and revise existing courses in the light of equal opportunities and assess the consultants and trainers used
8. To begin training needs analysis linked to policy and procedural change in (a) personal review; (b) criteria for promotion; (c) grievance and discipline; (d) harassment
9. To begin monitoring so that research into positive action programmes could begin in year two
10. To review access to existing internal and external courses and set targets for the following year.

## Translating the Plan into Action

The list of priorities was translated into the following action:

### 1. Senior commitment
*Action:* a one-day seminar for all senior management (heads of departments).
*Responsibility:* to be led by an external consultant, supported by the equal opportunities adviser and training staff.
*Total time:* one day.
*Completion:* by the end of month one.

### 2. Staff understanding
*Action:* two-hour lunchtime briefing sessions for all staff, conducted departmentally.
*Responsibility:* equal opportunities adviser and training staff.
*Total time:* ten days (40×2 hours).
*Completion:* by the end of month six.

### 3. Barriers to access

*Action:* (a) a three-day selection course for personnel staff;
(b) a three-day selection course for all managers due to interview within the following three months.
*Responsibility:* (a) to be conducted by external consultants;
(b) first four courses to be led by external consultants while training staff learn how to run them. Training staff then continue to run the rolling programme.
*Total time:* (a) three days;
(b) thirty days (10×3 days).
*Completion:* (a) by the end of month three;
(b) one course per month, ongoing.

### 4. Specialist knowledge

*Action:* (a) senior personnel staff to attend selected external courses;
(b) personnel to conduct briefings for senior management.
*Responsibility:* (a) external organization, eg, IPM;
(b) senior personnel staff assisted by the equal opportunities adviser.
*Total time:* (a) five days;
(b) one day.
*Completion:* (a) by the end of month nine;
 (b) by the end of the year.

### 5. Common core management module

*Action:* a two-day module for all management staff, from senior gradually down to junior.
*Responsibility:* (a) external consultant to assist training staff with the design;
(b) training staff to run the courses.
*Total time:* (a) ten days;
(b) 12 days (6×2 days).
*Completion:* ongoing – one course per month. Target 25 per cent of managers per year.

### 6. Training other tutors

*Action:* (a) one-day introductory workshop; (b) observation of lunchtime briefing sessions; (c) coaching sessions with training staff; (d) joint tutoring at sessions.
*Responsibility:* training staff.
*Total time:* two days.
*Completion:* by the end of month two.

### 7. Evaluation of existing courses

*Action:* (a) training staff observe selected consultant-run courses;
(b) material used on customer care; induction; supervisory skills and communication skills courses reviewed and revised;

(c) guidelines on equal opportunities to be prepared for tutors (external and internal).
*Responsibility:* training staff and equal opportunities adviser.
*Total time:* 20 days.
*Completion:* (a) by the end of month six;
 (b) by the end of the year;
 (c) by the end of month three.

### 8. Training needs analysis

*Action:* (a) produce a competency module for the four areas;
(b) identify key staff.
*Responsibility:* training staff and selected managers.
*Total time:* 20 days.
*Completion:* by the end of month nine.

### 9. Monitoring

*Action:* (a) design and implement a system;
(b) cascade information via managers to all staff.
*Responsibility:* (a) personnel staff and the equal opportunities adviser;
(b) equal opportunities adviser, personnel staff and managers.
*Total time:* not quantified.
*Completion:* by the end of the year.

### 10. Reviewing access to training

*Action:* (a) establish a training record system (linked to the monitoring system);
(b) produce statistical information on current access;
(c) prepare proposals for targets for access to future programmes.
*Responsibility:* (a) training staff;
(b) training staff;
(c) training staff, equal opportunities adviser and equal
 opportunities working group.
*Total time:* not quantified.
*Completion:* by the end of the year.

### Time and money

*Time:* the programme for the first year involved the training staff in a minimum of 100 person-days per year.
*Money:* the additional funding needed was calculated at a rate of £700 per day for external consultants' time and external courses, totalling £16,100.

These two items were added to the plan for approval but were not included in the published details.

## Tactics for Implementing your Training Plan

Once your plan is ready and approved, you can begin implementation. It is well worth planning in advance a tactical approach to the implementation of your training plan. You need to do this in order to:

- Deal with any barriers you might encounter
- Reduce the risk of failure
- Show that you have recognized the particular features of your organization.

### Tactical Steps

1. Involve all management levels at all stages – gain understanding if not active commitment
2. Establish credibility – try to show the benefits of EO training in terms of good practice
3. Identify training needs – use the experience and knowledge of managers and staff
4. Ensure that you have adequate resources – encourage members of staff to become involved in training, set up working groups to help you design training
5. Regularly consult with appropriate groups – include trade unions and members of the groups identified in your policy; build up momentum from below as well as from above
6. Choose appropriate levels and areas for maximum impact – but don't continue 'preaching only to the converted'
7. Choose your timing carefully – and make sure you and the policy move forward hand in hand
8. Explain *why* as well as *what* you are doing – make your objectives practical and clearly linked to expected change.

## Implementing Positive Action Programmes

As we have concentrated on the planning needed to establish the first year of any programme, we have not so far dealt in any detail with planning positive action programmes, as these are unlikely to be implemented in the initial stage. It is therefore worth spending some time looking at the additional factors you will need to take into account when you reach this stage. To check whether you are in a position to progress towards the implementation of positive action programmes, we suggest that you go through the following checklist.

CHECKLIST

1. Do you have monitoring information (gender/race/disability) on current staff and know where under-representation or lack of representation occurs?
2. Do you have a monitoring system for applicants for jobs and know where you have few/no applicants from EO groups applying or being appointed?
3. Is management sufficiently well informed/trained to provide support for positive action 'trainees'?
4. Have you established targets for each area of the organization (level of job and type of job) for:
   - women
   - black and ethnic minority staff
   - people with disabilities
   - other groups identified in your policy eg, age, sexual orientation?
5. Are non-discriminatory procedures in place governing recruitment, training, personal review (appraisal) and career progression?
6. Do you have physical access and support for people with mobility or other disabilities?
7. Do you have designated trainee posts suitable for positive action trainees?
8. Have job descriptions/person specifications been reviewed and revised to be non-discriminatory or positively amended to widen access (eg, experience alternatives to qualification requirements, flexible working, job share, etc)?
9. Have you conducted a training needs analysis (Chapter 3) amongst existing staff?

Our experience indicates that although not all of these elements need to be in place before you can undertake any positive action work, in practice it will be little more than a token gesture if they are not.

## Types of Positive Action Programmes

There are a number of different types of programme you can establish under the 'positive action' heading. These can be summarized as follows.

### Extending access to existing programmes
Can the criteria for access to courses be extended to include other grades? Can you set targets for access to sponsorship opportunities?

### Short in-house confidence building and career development courses
Short in-house courses are useful in a number of areas:

- Developing an understanding of existing systems and becoming more proficient at using them, eg, skills in job applications
- Raising awareness of behaviour at work and providing the skills to deal effectively with work situations, eg, assertion
- Informing and enabling people to make choices about their careers and the training and development opportunities available to them, eg, return-to-study courses
- Providing skills training for current jobs and for development purposes, eg, new technology; introduction to management; improving your English, etc.

Access to these courses is extended if people can self-select onto them rather than be nominated by managers.

### Access programmes

These are usually longer-term and linking formal training and work experience; they are designed to widen access to jobs. Some examples include:

- Day-release courses in vocational areas. These are often used to increase the skills of those who have no formal qualifications and are stuck in jobs with very limited career prospects. The courses are usually related to the skills needed at the next level or grade. They may or may not be linked to formal qualifications
- Positive action management trainee schemes, for existing staff to give greater access to management positions for under-represented groups. They often use a college-based qualification course, eg, a Diploma in Management Studies (DMS), linked to project-based work experience
- Pre-entry training leading to increased access for people who are not employees to apply for trainee posts or jobs in the organization. These are often run in conjunction with a college.

### Women returners schemes

These can be provided internally for employees returning from maternity leave. They consist of re-orientation and updating sessions with some elements of confidence building. Many employer-linked schemes are run by further and higher education institutions, with employers offering work-experience opportunities.

The type and range of positive action programmes your organization becomes involved in will depend on the general and specific factors we have raised and upon the resources available. Not only do external courses tend to be expensive, positive action trainees often need a lot of support from the organization, particularly if it involves people working in non-traditional areas. It is of debatable value to employ women apprentices on a building site and leaving them in glorious isolation! You do need a supportive climate, so we return again to the importance of training managers and other staff before you embark on positive action programmes.

A final word from experience: they will all take twice as long to set up as you think!

# 6 Encouraging People to Learn

    SUMMARY

- This chapter takes a brief look at motivation, and how far the various theories may be applied to training in general, and equal opportunities training in particular.
- It deals with some practical considerations about adult learning:
  - Theories of motivation
  - Why people go on training courses
  - Motivation and equal opportunities training
  - Difficulties
      challenging values and beliefs
      politics
  - Motivation to learn
  - How people learn.

## Motivation

Motivation is a complex issue for all those involved in training. What makes people take part in training activities? Once there, what encourages them to learn? After the event, what makes the learning stick?

These questions are regularly asked by people involved in training, and it may be helpful to look at them more broadly before focusing our attention on equal opportunities training, which has its own particular motivational problems.

## Getting Them There

Let us first of all take a brief and superficial look at some of the better known theories of motivation to see whether any of these are relevant to training.

> Individual motivation is determined by the extent to which the needs [an individual] brings to the job are matched by the incentives (such as rewards) provided by the organization. (Kakabadse *et al*, 1988, p.119).

However, what one individual regards as an incentive might be seen differently by another, so perceptions need to be taken into account.

These three variables of needs, incentives and perceptions, together with communication (Does the individual know what kinds of behaviour are rewarded?) and individual abilities, need to be taken into account when considering what motivates people.

There are several well-known theories of motivation, some (Alderfer, 1972; Maslow, 1954) looking at the individual and his or her needs, and others (Herzberg, 1966) looking at what organizations can do to motivate their workers. What they all say is that although people need to feel secure at work, to be paid well and have reasonable working conditions, something more than this is necessary to encourage them to work better; a sense of achievement, of a job worth doing, of personal growth, etc. In other words, improving working conditions or pay might reduce dissatisfaction and staff turnover, but will not motivate people to work better. The theories also take into account the fact that people hold expectations about the likelihood or probability that a behaviour on their part will lead to a particular outcome. These outcomes can be intrinsic (feeling good, sense of achievement), or extrinsic (praise, higher salary, etc). Expectations will be affected by the work itself, the work group, the environment and the culture of the organization. The closer the link between effort and outcome, the greater the motivation.

So how does this help us with equal opportunities training? First of all, the environment must be right: the organization must be, and must be seen to be, an equal opportunities organization. Second, the benefits to the organization as a whole of a more varied and flexible workforce which reflects the wider community need to be spelled out: that genuine equality of opportunity ultimately benefits all staff. Third, try to incorporate into your objectives reference to values which individuals might hold, such as fairness and justice.

## Why People Go on Training Courses

Why do people go on training courses? Here are the main reasons which have been given:

- To gain new skills
- To update or improve existing skills
- To extend knowledge
- To take a more objective view of work
- To share experiences, find out what others think, develop 'best practices'
- For personal development
- To enrich/enlarge the current job
- To aid career progression.

On the less positive side, people may also come along to air their knowledge, or to complain about the organization or their particular manager. Some may choose to come; some are told to come; others attend because it is company policy.

At the same time, we know that a lot of people do not choose to attend training activities, people who fail to see that there is anything in it for them. Why should this be? Are the benefits of training not clear? Do we need to make closer links between effective training and growth, advancement, achievement, etc? Problems of inertia often arise when training is allowed to happen in an *ad hoc* way; a planned programme is essential if you want to achieve the maximum benefit for your organization and the individuals within it. If the organization as a whole does not take training and development seriously, the chances are that individuals will not do so either.

## Motivation and Equal Opportunities Training

The list above does not include two objectives which underlie much equal opportunities training: increased awareness and attitude change. Rarely do people choose to attend training courses in order to change their attitudes, but this, stated or unstated, may be the wish of their managers or organizations. (The virtues of awareness as opposed to behavioural training are considered in Chapter 4, but it is important to realize that, however the subject of equal opportunities is treated, people will either directly or indirectly be asked to consider their existing attitudes, and there will inevitably be knock-on emotional effects. Guilt and/or resentment are likely to affect some of your trainees.)

### Difficulties

Equal opportunities is a topic about which people have strong feelings, and training may question or at least bring to the surface values and beliefs which may be an intrinsic part of a person's make-up and yet are rarely consciously thought about. This can be a painful process, in which the training course may only be the start of a journey of self-knowledge, and it is important to build in some kind of follow-on training or advisory sessions so that people can ask questions about the sort of things which may only occur to them some time after they have begun to think about their attitudes. Again, people may be anxious lest they be judged morally 'wrong', hesitant to express views which they feel they should not hold. They may well find it helpful to have someone with whom they can talk over concerns on a one-to-one basis rather than as a member of a group.

Another problem is that equal opportunities has all too often been used as a political football, and the trainer must ensure that party politics are avoided. Some people attend training events in order to score political points and they need careful handling; they may be well informed and the skilled trainer may be able to make use of this information while emphasizing the crucial aims of fairness and legal requirements.

There are many ways in which trainers can persuade people to attend training courses. In order to get the course filled, trainers have been known to resort to such bribes as: it will do you good to have a day away from the office/the refreshments are always good/etc! Once there, it is up to you as a trainer to make sure that the course meets its objectives, keeps the attention and interest of the people on it, and provides long-lasting and beneficial results.

## Keeping Them There – The Training Event

'You can send people off on as many courses as you like; it doesn't mean they are going to come back having learned anything' (Daedal Training, undated).

'Prisoners', 'passengers', 'participants' and 'protestors' are categories suggested by Clive Hook (1990), examples of which can be found on most training courses. The following passage is based on his ideas.

'Prisoners' have been told to come; they do not want to be there and they do not intend to learn anything. This may be stated at the start of the course, or it may become apparent from body language and lack of involvement in exercises and discussion as the course progresses.

'Passengers' may be there because it's better than work or because they feel that perhaps they ought; they may believe that equal opportunities is about fairness, which they support, but that people are basically fair and it is not necessary to go to special lengths to enforce this. Or they may know that the law requires certain standards of behaviour and they realize the importance of being well informed; they will go along with the majority view but are unlikely to contribute anything themselves. They will respond to reason, but not to preaching.

'Participants' are likely to be in sympathy with the aims of the training and willing to learn more; they will be enthusiastic and willing to contribute; their support can be enlisted to encourage the others.

'Protestors' may be noisy prisoners, and it takes skill and energy to cope with the sort of person who argues every point with you. If you try to deal adequately with the protestor, you run the risk of losing the rest of the group. Again, if you have sufficient participants and passengers you may be able to use them to stimulate a more constructive discussion; failing that you, may have to give priority to the needs of the majority and arrange to have a separate discussion with the protestors. Another type of protestor, equally difficult to deal with, uses the opportunity of being with a group to protest about his or her manager, organization, or lot in life generally. Again, the skilled trainer will try to keep discussion relevant and positive without alienating the protestor.

Pitching the level of the training activity can be difficult if the course is made up of a mixture of the interested and fairly knowledgeable and the uninterested or hostile. In my own organization, a half-day seminar intended to de-mystify equal opportunities was offered to all those with staff working for them, but in the event was attended largely by personnel specialists whose needs were rather different from those for whom the course was originally intended. The trainer had a difficult task keeping the personnel officers motivated while ensuring that the less knowledge-able supervisors were not lost.

Much depends on how people are selected to attend training sessions; if they volunteer themselves, they are likely to be more or less committed anyway, in which case you might consider using them to cascade the learning down to other, less committed, people. Equal opportunity issues are not always best discussed in a formal training course – a great deal of valuable learning can take place on the job or during informal discussions among colleagues. Equipping suitable 'volunteers' with the right information and some discussion-leading skills can be an extremely useful tool in encouraging learning about equal opportunities. An example of a cascade awareness training approach used by the University of Southampton is given in the appendix.

Any group which has been told it must attend a course is likely to contain some prisoners and protestors. It is rarely advisable to make a course compulsory, but there are times when it is necessary, mostly because of legal requirements. The majority of organizations find that training is most effective when it supports a previously agreed policy and, if a stick is needed, one relating specifically to the institution is likely to have more effect than a more distant law. All staff need to know what they must and must not do, and though for some it may be enough for them to read the appropriate regulations, for other staff something more is needed. They must be told that certain standards of behaviour are required, regardless of their own personal views.

If protesters are protesting about equal opportunities rather than training in general they may respond better to the incorporation of equal opportunities training into other, more general courses. This will avoid the initial negative reactions and introduce equal opportunities (which need not be called such) at relevant points during the programme when the learner is likely to be more receptive (see also Chapter 4).

## How People Learn

A great deal has been written about the theory of learning, and all we will attempt to do here is to present some practical considerations for the trainer to bear in mind.

All learning is more effective when people wish to participate in it and compulsory training should be used as little as possible. Too many people are allowed to think that training performs a punitive function, that if they are invited to attend a course they have somehow failed. It is important to separate the inadequate performance from the person and to emphasize the role of training as a positive tool to help someone develop skills or improve performance, or learn to cope better with change.

All those involved in training should be aware that:

- Adults need to want to learn
- Adults need to see that there is something in it for them
- They need to see the relevance of the activity – this is best discussed and jointly agreed beforehand
- The new learning must fit in with what they already know
- Adults usually learn best by doing (rather than being told) in a relaxed and relatively informal environment
- The training methods used should be appropriate to both subject and learners
- Trainees should have confidence in the trainer
- Feedback is necessary so that people know how they are doing. Criticism should be positive and constructive
- Success is a greater motivator than failure.

Try to bear these factors in mind next time you plan a training activity. Another important point to remember is that, just as trainers have different styles, so too do learners. Some learn best by being told, some by trial and error, some by imitation and others by thinking. It will not be possible to satisfy all needs during a group training activity, but you should try to devise approaches which take different learning styles into account, so that a certain amount of telling is followed by some practical exercises, for example.

# 7 Running Equal Opportunities Training Events

 SUMMARY

- This chapter looks at the practical aspects of running equal opportunities training events. It includes:
  - Integrating equal opportunities
  - Setting objectives
  - Useful training methods
  - Selecting material
  - Language and behaviour in the course room
  - Facing challenges
  - Confidentiality
- It contains examples of material to use and some tried and tested ways of running effective courses.

This chapter gets you into the training room at last! If you have followed the processes we have recommended throughout the book you should be very well equipped for this moment. You should know who you are training, what their needs are and when and how you are training them. The design and running of the course are, however, the most visible parts of the process and thus are of key importance.

The sequence we intend to follow in this chapter is to look at the process of:

- Raising the issues
- Setting objectives
- Selecting methods
- Selecting material
- Language and behaviour
- Dealing with challenges
- Confidentiality

## Equal Opportunities in the Course – Where Does it Go?

In our experience, the courses which work least well are those which pre-date the equal opportunities policy, which continue as before except that they suddenly develop a slot called 'equal opportunities' somewhere in their programme. This makes it easy for people to perceive it as a marginal issue and makes it virtually impossible for them to apply it to any of the other skills they are there to develop.

We therefore recommend that the structure, material and methodologies you use allow the issues raised by equal opportunities to be addressed throughout the course in a variety of contexts. This allows understanding to build step-by-step and, most importantly, to be usable back in the workplace.

## Gender, Race and Disability

There has been some debate about whether the issues of race, gender and disability should be dealt with in separate training courses or all treated as generic equal opportunities issues. Although we have encountered both models, the most effective approach seems to be one which combines the two. Caution needs to be exercised if you treat the issues as separate from each other because of course people with disabilities can also be women and/or black; black women can be subject to racism and sexism and with this approach you can end up so deeply involved in the nature of the issue that you lose sight of the people involved. Conversely, the other approach can lead to assumptions being made that one set of standard measures solves all problems when the needs of women may be very different from those of a white male with visual impairment, for example.

On the whole it seems to work best if you follow this approach:

- Information training           all groups discussed
- Management/staff training to     all groups discussed
  implement the policy
- Management/staff training       groups dealt with separately
  to support positive action
  programmes for specific
  groups
- Positive action programmes     groups dealt with separately.

## Setting Objectives

Some points to remember:

- Your objectives will obviously relate to the needs you have identified; people become quite irritated if they have contributed to the assessment of needs and then attend a 'bought-in course' which appears to have only a tenuous connection to these.
- Your objectives should reflect the skills, knowledge and observable behaviours to be developed. These then provide you, the course participants and subsequently their managers, with clear pointers against which their progress can be measured.
- It is usually not terribly useful to include specific references to attitudes towards equal opportunities in your objectives; it can deter people and is impossible to measure. People can learn the 'jargon' or stay quiet and you will have no idea what they are really thinking. As a sub-text on the course, you can of course show positive alternatives to negative attitudes and create the circumstances that might encourage people to change, but it is usually as well not to announce this in advance.
- Well defined and clearly expressed objectives get you a long way towards helping to identify appropriate methods.
- You should not have too many objectives; more than five or six and you have probably got more than one course.

It might be useful to look at an example of objective-setting for a selection skills course and then take these forward into identifying methods of training; one is given in Figure 7.1.

---

OBJECTIVES FOR A THREE-DAY SELECTION SKILLS COURSE

At the end of the course the participants will be able to:

1. Demonstrate through a number of exercises and quizzes that they understand the meaning of the main equality concepts in recruitment, ie, discrimination, positive action, GOQs, targets and quotas.
2. Design a non-discriminatory person specification which accurately reflects the requirements of a particular job description.
3. Draw up a shortlist for interview based on the person specification and demonstrate an ability to identify transferable skills.
4. Demonstrate that by using appropriate and non-discriminatory questioning techniques, listening and accurate note-taking, they can conduct an interview in which they gather sufficient information to enable a fair decision to be made on recruitment.
5. Demonstrate that the criteria they have used for final selection are fair and show how each candidate has been measured against them.

---

**Figure 7.1** *An example of objective-setting for a selection skills course*

As you will see, these objectives have been expressed in terms which are measurable and give participants a clear picture of what they are there to learn.

Before looking at the methods best suited to achieve these objectives, it may be helpful to look at training methods in general.

# Training Methods

It is worth spending some time thinking about the methods which are most likely to work in helping people to learn about equal opportunities. In common with all other training, you will want to use as wide a range as possible to add interest and to allow a variety of opportunities for practice.

## What to Bear in Mind when Choosing Methods

- Are they the best way of achieving your objectives?
- Are you able to use them comfortably?
- Are they consistent with your participants' expectations?
- Are they most appropriate for knowledge, skill or behavioural learning?

**Best Methods?**

In general we have found that *what works best is* :

| | |
|---|---|
| PARTICIPATIVE | – active not passive learning |
| PRACTICAL | – dealing with real working situations and problems |
| MULTI-FORM | – learning points reinforced and practised in a variety of settings. |

*What works less well is* :

| | |
|---|---|
| DIRECTIVE | – there is only one right answer – mine! |
| THEORETICAL | – either too many facts and figures or exercises requiring too much of a conceptual leap to apply to real life situations |
| EXPERIENTIAL | – attempting to make people feel what it is like to be discriminated against. |

*Participative, practical and multi-form*
In this set of methods we would include:

| | |
|---|---|
| Panel/small group discussions | knowledge learning |
| Debates | knowledge learning |
| Quizzes | knowledge learning |
| Question and answer sessions | knowledge learning |
| Brainstorming | knowledge learning |
| Problem solving groups/exercises | applying knowledge |
| Case studies | applying knowledge |
| 'Real life simulations', eg, interviews | skills/behaviour |
| Trigger films | knowledge/skills |
| Role play | skills/behaviour |
| Exercises based on real decisions | knowledge/skills |

*Directive, theoretical and experiential*
In this set of methods we would include:

| | |
|---|---|
| Reading | knowledge learning |
| Lectures | knowledge learning |
| Simulations of artificial situations | skills/behaviour |
| Games unrelated to work, eg, Lego | skills/behaviour |
| Films/videos | knowledge learning |
| T-groups, fish-bowl exercises | behaviour/attitudes |

NB – reading, lectures and films and videos are of course all valid and often useful training methods, but unless followed up by extensive feedback sessions, they are a passive experience unmeasurable in terms of learning. Games, simulations and T-group encounter sessions, although they can be a powerful experience, need to be treated with care unless you are an expert in human behaviour and can de-brief the experience successfully. (Examples of unsuccessful sessions are shown in Figure 7.2.) You may well unearth all sorts of attitudes, emotions and problems but unless you know what to do with them afterwards, this can be a negative experience for all concerned.

---

UNSUCCESSFUL SESSIONS

1.  A course on 'Men and Women Working Together' involved use of the fishbowl exercise with first women and then men talking together about their feelings about work, family, friends, etc. The men ended up so depressed about their scope for an emotional life that the remainder of the course was spent with the women in their traditional role providing comfort, counselling and advice to their male colleagues. Neither found it a positive event.

2.  An anti-racism course attempted to give white participants some experience of the effects of discrimination. Signs in the training room were written in Arabic; the 'in-group' were briefed to use particular behaviours and gestures which the 'excluded' group would not be able to understand. Conventional hierarchies were reversed. Half the course ended up in uncontained mirth, the other in furious hostility; the experience of discrimination was totally lost in the proceedings.

---

**Figure 7.2** *Some examples of unsuccessful sessions*

NB – experiential learning of the sort we have described is easier to use on positive action courses where participants form a more homogeneous group and often have a longer period to build up trust.

## Applying Methods to a Programme

We will now look at the course we used as an example of objective-setting to show how these were translated into a programme and which methods were selected for each key topic; the course is summarized in Figure 7.3.

**Figure 7.3** *An example of methods used in a selection skills course*

PROGRAMME FOR A THREE-DAY SELECTION SKILLS COURSE

| *Topic* | *Method* |
|---|---|
| FRAMEWORK | |
| 1. EO legislation relating to recruitment. Company policy | Précis of legislation and copy of company policy. Twenty-point questionnaire completed individually |
| PROCESS OF RECRUITMENT | |
| 2. Job description | Small group exercise identifying possible discriminatory features in a selection of ten job descriptions |
| 3. Person specification | Small group work to produce a person specification based on a company job description and pro-forma |
| 4. Advertisements | Two groups, one to write the advertisement for above job designed to encourage EO groups to apply, one to write one to discourage. Full group review |
| 5. Shortlists | Small group exercise to select shortlist from ten 'mock' application forms. |
| 6. Monitoring | Short lecture on the monitoring scheme; Q and A session |
| THE INTERVIEW | |
| 7. Function | Full group discussion based on handout |
| 8. Structure | Alternative models given by tutor. Panels asked to adopt one |
| 9. Questioning | Handout on question types. Trigger film of an interview; participants asked to identify each question type used |
| 10. Listening | 'Baton' listening exercise. Full group brainstorm on good listening |
| 11. Note-taking | Tape of interview played and participants take notes; tape stopped at intervals and questions asked on facts |
| 12. EO adherence | Panels to devise six questions to test interviewees' support for the equal opportunities policy |

| 13. Interview practice | Four 20-minute videoed interviews with 'guinea-pigs'. Feedback using tutor observation and video extracts |
|---|---|
| DECISION-MAKING | |
| 14. Individual | Individual exercise to convert notes onto a pro-forma assessing candidates' suitability against each item on the person specification |
| 15. Group | Panel discussion to reach concensus on candidate rating |
| 16. Review evidence | Panels present and justify evidence for ratings to tutor panel |
| 17. Final selection | Case study notes on six candidates. Small group decision on who to select |
| FOLLOW-UP | |
| 18. References | Lecturette followed by Q and A session |
| 19. Medicals | Ditto |
| 20. Job offers | Ditto |

**Review of Methods**

As this course is predominantly about the development of skills, the methods chosen are highly participatory. A significant portion of the time is spent on the role-played interviews, videoed so that participants can practise and monitor their own developing skills. The knowledge content is conveyed by exercises, eg, 20 questions which require the participants to find out the information rather than being told. The exercises are practical ones, simulating the process of activities they will need to follow when recruiting in 'real life', enabling learning to be absorbed more easily. The methods cover as wide a range as possible to provide interest.

# Incorporating Equal Opportunities

Although the course begins by setting the legal framework, equal opportunities is interwoven through the whole course. Attitudes to equal opportunities are likely to be raised throughout the process but there is no point at which people are 'preached at'. The issues addressed are outlined below:

### Job descriptions

Ensuring that requirements for jobs are not discriminatory; assessing whether jobs can be designed to be more accessible to equal opportunities groups.

### Person specifications

Producing fair and objective criteria for selection; reducing reliance on 'acceptability to the existing team' or other non-job-related factors.

### Advertisements

Identifying GOQs; how to use positive encouragement to apply; possible indirect discrimination in advertising.

### Short-listing

Using fair criteria; looking for transferable skills; avoiding stereotypes.

### Monitoring

Why there is a policy; the role of recruitment in promoting equal access.

### The interview

The importance of appointing the best person for the job and not relying on prejudice and assumptions; gathering information rather than making decisions during the interview; not asking discriminatory questions; assessing whether new appointees will support the policy.

### Decision-making

Assessing evidence against criteria, not personal likes/dislikes; justifying the fairness of the selection decision.

### Follow up

Equality of pay and conditions.

## Selecting Material

It has been our experience that there is not a great deal of commercially available training material which addresses equal opportunities issues. This does not of course mean that you cannot use it but it may require some additions and amendments to bring it into line with the issues you want to raise. An exercise on team building can, for example, be developed to include gender and race; a customer care case study can be extended to include issues raised if your customer has a disability or does not speak English as a first language. In most of the courses we have run, we have found that writing our own material has proved more successful. Research in your own organization, while conducting your training needs analysis, for example, will often give you enough examples and incidents to produce case studies and role plays for a multiplicity of courses. One advantage of using your own material is that you can avoid using stereotypes, you can ensure that the material is gender-neutral and that it reflects the priorities and procedures of your own organization.

While we have given details of some commercially available material in the appendix, to get you started on writing your own we have suggested, in Figure 7.4, some short scenarios which you can expand and adapt for use in your own organization. They can be used for case studies or role plays to raise issues of procedures and practice (and underlying attitudes).

**Figure 7.4** *Scenarios for case studies and role plays*

Questions should focus on the action managers/staff would take in these circumstances.

1. A white member of the public refuses to deal with a black member of staff at the counter and is using racist and abusive language.
2. You hear a male lecturer consistently address women students and staff as 'dear'. Some have said that they find this patronizing.
3. A woman member of staff complains to you that she has been sexually harassed.
4. You have recently been appointed to head a department of 50 people. You are concerned that there are only two black women in it, both in the lowest grade. You want to find out why.
5. A member of staff comes to you to say that the staff are not happy with John making the tea as they think he is gay and they are worried about AIDS.
6. You have been asked to produce a strategy to increase the number of women recruited into your department over the next five years.
7. You have been asked to identify a post suitable for a wheelchair user.
8. A black member of staff accuses you of racism when you initiate disciplinary action for poor time-keeping.
9. A trade union representative asks you to explain your promotion criteria as it seems that women are not being promoted although they say that they are as well qualified and experienced as the men.
10. A black client complains to you that your service is discriminatory as they have been unable to get a grant/business loan/house (fill in your own service).
11. You are a male manager at an all-male departmental/heads meeting when the nature of the discussion makes it clear that they are not going to take equal opportunities issues seriously.
12. You need to plan to brief your team that a new recruit with a hearing disability is soon to join you.

The scenarios can be used in courses ranging from management to communications and from team building to disciplinary; just check that you know the answers!

## Language and Behaviour in the Course Room

As the trainer you have an important part to play in demonstrating the behaviour and use of language you want your participants to adopt. If you constantly allow men to interrupt or dominate sessions, or you refer to women as 'girls', or you continue to use gender-specific terms like 'man management', your participants will soon get the message (even if unintended) that the commitment to equal opportunities is merely cosmetic.

Language is obviously important in helping to define how people are viewed; terms like 'man management' result in an invisible female workforce and reinforce the impression that women workers are of no importance. Incidentally, we have yet to meet any women who are convinced or flattered by the assertion that the word 'man' includes them! In considering language and behaviour we are not recommending a rigid 'politically correct' approach but suggesting that how you behave towards and speak to people should reflect how people wish to be treated rather than your or society's view of how they should be. This can always be determined by asking them! We recommend, therefore, that you:

- Set the standards of language and behaviour for the course as part of your introduction.
- Use gender-neutral terms; 'workforce' and 'staffing' rather than 'manpower' and 'manning'.
- Use terms which confer dignity and reflect how people have indicated they wish to be addressed, eg, 'black', not 'coloured'; 'people with disabilities', rather than 'disabled people'; 'women', rather than 'girls'; 'lesbian and gay men', not homosexuals.
- Make it clear that discriminatory comments and jokes are offensive. We have found it useful to challenge derogatory remarks by saying, 'Could you tell us why you think...?', followed by, 'Could you tell us your evidence for...?'. Invite contributions from other course members but be careful not to allow women to take sole responsibility for challenging sexist remarks or black people for racist remarks.
- Challenge stereotypes, initially by excluding them from your own material but also if necessary by using quick exercises like the following:

- Have two flipcharts, one with 'all men are good at' and one with 'all men are hopeless at' written at the top. Conduct a quick brainstorm for appropriate words for each list. At the end of two minutes, ask all participants (including women) to select the three from each that most apply to them. The resulting mixture should effectively start a discussion about the appropriateness of stereotypes.

● On a final lighter note...if faced by accusations that equal opportunities has somehow ruined the unchanging purity of the English language by introducing terms like 'Ms' and 'Chair' instead of 'Chairman', make sure you have memorized some of the more obscure Shakespearean passages – unchanging indeed!

We have summarized our tips on running courses in Figure 7.5

**Figure 7.5** *Dos and don'ts on training courses*

---

**DOs**

1. Avoid stereotypes in case studies and examples
2. Use he and she (or they)
3. Use pair and small group work to increase the opportunity for everyone to participate
4. Occasionally elect spokespersons for group feedback who are not from the majority group of course participants, rather than always allowing self-selection
5. Challenge discriminatory language or behaviour, explaining why you are doing so
6. Be a role model for participants in your language and behaviour
7. Practise defending your own beliefs; rehearse your responses to negativity or hostility
8. At least initially work with someone else for support; male/female, black/white partnerships are often effective as they challenge the 'vested interest of the trainer' accusations

**DON'Ts**

1. Use examples where all managers are male, all secretaries are female
2. Use gender-specific terms
3. Use too much large group work where men can tend to dominate or too many 'Lego'-type games where men also tend to think they are the natural leaders because technical skills are required (unless of course you wish to demonstrate stereotypical behaviour)
4. Use participants as spokespersons for the whole of their gender or race, eg, 'Sue, you are a woman manager, tell us how women managers feel about...'

---

5. Jump down peoples' throats if they use out-dated expressions about EO, eg, it used to be polite to describe people as 'coloured' rather than 'black'. Participants need to know how and why this has changed
6. Allow offensive anti-equal opportunities statements to be made on the basis that training courses are confidential and people should be allowed to air their views. People need to be free to question and clarify their own beliefs but not at the expense of others
7. Be drawn into colluding, particularly if you are a male trainer, even if you do initially feel isolated
8. Expect to be universally popular!

## Facing Challenges

You are very likely at some stage in your training to face arguments against equal opportunities, probably for one or more of the following reasons:

- People believe the myths about what it is and consequently feel threatened (women will be getting all the jobs)
- They believe that it is a political issue and they disagree with the perceived politics behind it
- They find it difficult to recognize or objectively review the values and beliefs they have grown up with (as do we all!) and feel these are under attack
- They believe that they would never discriminate anyway and that it is therefore irrelevant for them (the 'some of my best friends are...' argument)
- They think that it is going to produce a lot more work for them
- Plus any other combination you can think of!

Incidentally, you would be mistaken if you thought these challenges would only come from white men.

### Useful Responses

You need to be prepared with a range of arguments – to be presented calmly – in support of equal opportunities. We have suggested a few below that you may wish to use but you will undoubtedly be able to add to this as your experience of implementation develops.

- If is not about positive discrimination, it does not offer favouritism or unfair advantage (see Chapter 1)

- It is not a party political issue; organizations of all political complexions have adopted equal opportunities policies: Conservative- and Labour-led local authorities, the Civil Service and major commercial organizations such as BP and Marks & Spencer
- Natural justice suggests that although human beings possess a range of different culturally-determined values, no particular set is superior to any other. Even if not born equal, people are entitled to an equal and fair opportunity to succeed
- The advantages accruing from the adoption of a policy are likely to extend beyond the 'equal opportunities' groups. Flexible working practices can be of benefit to all: paternity leave is unlikely without the establishment of good maternity leave provision; objective promotion criteria may also benefit previously disadvantaged men
- It makes economic and commercial good sense. An organization is more likely to thrive if it selects the best people for its jobs rather than recruiting solely in its own image. Talent is distributed among a wide section of the population! An organization is likely to offer a better service or product if its clients/customers are reflected in its workforce
- The impact of demographic change means that organizations can not always rely on being able to recruit from a pool of young white male school or college leavers (should they have wished do so in the first place)
- The adoption of good equal opportunities practice impacts upon practice and procedure and generally makes it more effective. Recruitment will be done more systematically; interviewers will be trained, possibly for the first time; working relationships will become more 'professional'; under-utilized talent will be identified and developed through personal review or appraisal schemes

and finally:

- it is *the law* and company policy requires compliance (it may even be an element of an employee's contract).

## Confidentiality on the Course

The beauty of attending a course it that you can learn in private, make mistakes, make a fool of yourself, all without judgements affecting your job or career. Is this true of equal opportunities? Well yes, up to a point. What happens however, if you have a declared racist on your selection skills course who is going to return unchanged to interviewing? As the trainer you now have evidence that this person will continue to discriminate, contrary to company policy. Can you maintain the confidentiality of the training room? If you do not, and announce at the beginning that you will not be able to do so in certain circumstances, do you spend the course time looking at rows of clams?

Having got you to this point we are afraid that we are about to say that we have no real solution to this dilemma apart from saying that it is an issue you should have discussed in advance and, if possible, on which you should have reached some agreed consistent policy.

It may be useful to quote a few examples of action that other organizations have taken in these circumstances (these all relate to recruitment interviewing):

- A training contract for selection skills requiring course participants to be able to demonstrate their competency in the classroom before being authorized to conduct interviews in their job
- The ability to effectively implement the policy was written into the personal review scheme. People therefore knew that it was a requirement of their job before they attended training courses; it was their manager's, rather than the trainer's, responsibility to assess this and to take necessary action
- Course participants were asked to assess for themselves whether they felt competent to conduct interviews after the training course. Further training was available for those who decided they needed it
- No one was allowed to interview without more experienced interviewers on the panel
- Trainers were asked to notify the personnel department of participants who they felt had not fully demonstrated their ability to interview fairly. The personnel department then monitored the conduct of the participants' first real interviews.

# 8    Is your Training Effective?

                SUMMARY

● Validation and evaluation are complementary activities which need to be
  incorporated into the overall training plan, and which must be preceded by setting
  clear and achievable objectives. This chapter covers:
  – establishing a baseline
  – five key questions
  – measuring training effectiveness
  – validation
  – evaluation.

## Definitions

In this book we use the term 'validation' to mean the assessment of the
training event in relation to its objectives – has it achieved what it set out
to achieve? 'Evaluation' assesses the effects of the training on later
performance and whether any improved standard has been maintained.

## Establishing a Baseline

Both activities need to be incorporated into the overall training plan, and
both rely on the setting of clear objectives at an early stage. In addition,

it is important to establish the starting point or baseline so that you can plan an appropriate approach and evaluate both short- and longer-term benefits. The 'prisoner' with no prior interest in equal opportunities, who later grudgingly admitted that perhaps there was something in it, may have come much further than the 'participant' who was already concerned about unfair employment practices and went away determined to do something about them.

The baseline will tell you the extent of your organization's commitment to and understanding of equal opportunities (does it have a policy, is a commitment to equal opportunities incorporated into the strategic plan, what are its public pronouncements, how far are these supported by senior management?). It will also tell you how much all of this is understood by the staff (see Chapter 3, page 38, for a salutary case history!). Establishing how much knowledge and understanding already exists is part of the training needs analysis process, discussed in Chapter 3. This procedure will prepare the ground for the post-training evaluation and give you the means to measure change.

## Five Key Questions

For both validation and evaluation, trainers need to ask themselves five key questions: *why, what, how, who* and *when*. Each question needs to take into account the context in which the training is taking place – the nature of the organization, staff profile, your role as trainer, resources available, etc.

*Why* might seem obvious to you, but it is useful to have it clear in your own mind so that you can respond to questions. For the organization, an investment in training requires some evidence of returns. Training personnel need evidence by which to plan future training, or modify the existing programme. Learners need to know how they are progressing.

*What*, precisely, are you trying to assess? Clearly, you will need to refer back to your objectives. Try to differentiate between how the course was presented and received from its effects on performance.

On the course, *who* is usually the trainer or the training manager. Later evaluation could in theory involve a number of people – the trainer, the manager, the personnel officer, even other members of staff or the public. A course on customer care for reception staff, for example, might be evaluated by means of questions to members of the public about the quality of service, or by monitoring complaints, although without a means of identifying respondents it will not be possible to separate equal opportunities generally from the overall standard of service. The criteria to consider when deciding who should evaluate are acceptability and effectiveness, and both will be affected by what you have chosen to evaluate.

*When* has already been mentioned; the ideal would be regularly over a period of time, but this is unlikely to be feasible for most hard-worked trainers. Reactions from participants at the time of the training are valuable, particularly in terms of its immediate impact – the content and how it related to the objectives, the overall balance of the programme, the presentation, and methods used. Asking for feedback also helps to increase motivation by making participants feel they have some ownership of the training and that their comments might affect future plans. However, these comments will be subjective; many objective tests carried out at this time are likely to be a test of memory than of real learning; tests on the longer-term effects of the training should take place at a later date.

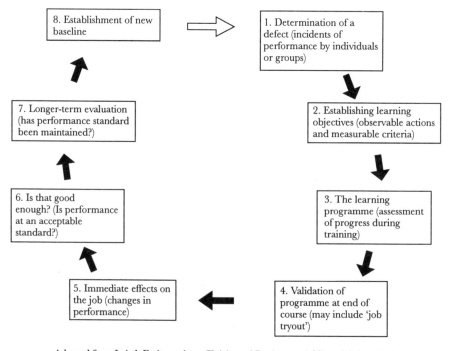

Adapted from Laird, D *Approaches to Training and Development*, Addison-Wesley, 1978.

**Figure 8.1** *Measuring training effectiveness*

Evaluation is a means of checking how far any improved standard has been maintained and therefore needs to take place some time after the event. It helps the trainer to assess the real benefits of the training to the organization, and whether the training methods used were the most effective.

*How* will be considered in more detail. All measures of training effectiveness need to be sound and objective, administratively convenient and acceptable. Ideally, this should be a continuous process so that as the learning curve begins to drop, remedial training takes place. Figure 8.1 shows the cyclical nature of measuring training effectiveness.

# Validation

### On or soon after the course

Validation carried out on the course is usually easy to administer, acceptable, and you can be sure of getting a good rate of response. It can be carried out in a number of different ways:

- As an on-going part of the training activity. The trainer will be constantly alert to the effectiveness of the different parts of the programme
- More formally, by verbal or written questions, or through practical exercises, at various points in the programme
- Through the views of the learners, at the end of the programme, both verbally and in written form. Written comments are very often anonymous, so that trainees can express their opinions more freely. A sample form is given in Figure 8.2.

**Figure 8.2** *An example of a course assessment sheet*

---

**Borough of Cranford Housing Department**

COURSE ASSESSMENT SHEET

*Course:*                                                                       *Date:*

1. What was your objective in attending?

2. Was that objective met? If not, please state reasons

3. What was the most helpful part of the course?

4. What aspects could be altered or improved?

---

5. How would you rate the course overall?

*Excellent*           *Very Good*         *Good*          *Average*          *Poor*

6. Any other comments?

*Please return to Chris Smith, Training Department.*

A variation on this approach is to ask trainees to write brief comments on Post-it notes which can then be 'posted' onto sheets of flip-chart paper with headings such as 'liked most', 'liked least', 'needed more on', 'needed less on', 'success in meeting objectives'.

### Action plans

You can also begin to look at the longer-term effects of the training by asking trainees to fill in an action plan at the end of the course, writing down changes which they plan to make as a result of what they have learned. It is a good idea to ask trainees to work in pairs or small groups so that they will have support from colleagues in carrying out the action plans. Examples of simple and more complex action sheets are given in Figures 8.3 and 8.4.

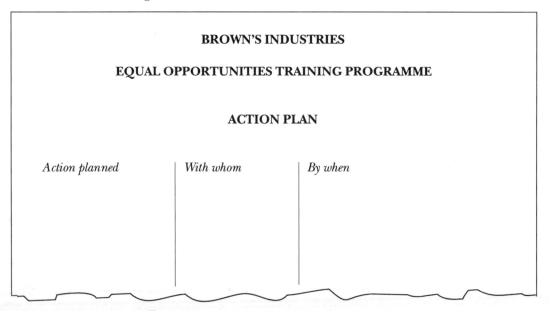

**Figure 8.3** *An example of a simple action plan*

---

**BROWN'S INDUSTRIES**

**EQUAL OPPORTUNITIES TRAINING PROGRAMME**

SELECTION SKILLS COURSE

Now that you have finished this course, it's time to think about putting your learning to use. Please use these columns to estimate when you hope to apply the course objectives listed on the left:

| | always | I plan to do this | | never | I failed to achieve this objective |
| | | often | sometimes | | |
|---|---|---|---|---|---|
| 1. Revise application forms | | | | | |
| 2. Ensure that job descriptions and person specifications are based on relevant, objective criteria | | | | | |
| 3. Ensure that I avoid questions which could be directly or indirectly discriminatory | | | | | |
| etc. | | | | | |

**Figure 8.4** *An example of a more complex action plan*

You may decide to keep a copy of the action sheets yourself in order to carry out later evaluation; if so, make sure that the reason you are doing this is made clear to the group, otherwise you may encounter anxiety and resentment.

A second questionnaire to be sent out two or three months after the course may then be personalized, based on individual action plans, or it may in more general terms ask for comments on any changes introduced or noted as a result of the training. An example of a more general follow-up questionnaire is given in Figure 8.5.

**Figure 8.5** *An example of a general follow-up questionnaire*

---

### UNIVERSITY OF LONDON

### ACADEMIC MANAGEMENT PROGRAMME 5–10 APRIL 1992

EVALUATION PART II

This questionnaire is designed firstly to help you to review the learning you achieved during the Academic Management Programme held in April this year, and secondly to give me an understanding of the longer-term benefits of the course, and any omissions, to help with future planning. If you have the time you might find it useful to ask any colleagues you named in your action plans for their comments.

**Review of Learning**

What were your most important learning objectives or training needs when you came on the course? Please describe these briefly and on the associated scale indicate how far these were met:

|     | Not<br>at<br>all |   |   |   | Fully |
| --- | --- | --- | --- | --- | --- |
| a)  | 1 | 2 | 3 | 4 | 5 |
| b)  | 1 | 2 | 3 | 4 | 5 |
| c)  | 1 | 2 | 3 | 4 | 5 |
| d)  | 1 | 2 | 3 | 4 | 5 |

Did any other significant learning points, not previously identified, occur on the course? If so, please identify them.

Have you made any changes to the way you manage your department as a result of the course? If so, please give examples and indicate how these contribute to the effectiveness of the department.

What further learning objectives or training needs related to workshop topics remain to be met?

Thank you for completing the questionnaire. Please return it to the Training and Development Unit...

---

# Evaluation

The improvement of skills as a result of training is relatively easy to assess compared with the assessment of increased awareness and attitude change and their effect on performance. However, tests can be devised for both and examples are given at the end of this chapter.

Some skills relating to equal opportunities can be isolated and evaluated – interviewing skills for example. You can monitor performance the next time trainees are involved in interviewing by observation, questioning, or examination of written records, checking such things as the establishment of objective, relevant criteria, the avoidance of questions which might be seen as directly or indirectly discriminatory, and the keeping of records about reasons for rejection.

If you have been able to establish an organizational baseline then you will have something to measure improvements against – data from monitoring, number of complaints, or personnel records on such things as absenteeism or staff turnover. You may need help from a statistician or data analyst in interpreting data. Most trainers with limited resources will need to restrict their investigations to the most critical aspects of the training. Evaluation of senior staff can be difficult (how do you evaluate the quality of decision-making, for example?) and, depending upon your position in the organization, you may need to enlist the help of a more senior member of staff. Appropriate questions may also be asked during the appraisal interview, for example.

## Methods of Validation and Evaluation

There are many different methods of measuring the effects of learning on performance; the one you choose will depend upon what you are trying to measure – skills, knowledge, or attitude. *Skills* can be tested by self-appraisal, by oral, written or practical tests, by observation 'on-the-job', or by examination of the outcomes, eg, number of complaints. *Knowledge* is usually tested orally, or in writing; examples are given in Figure 8.6. *Attitude* and attitude change may be tested by subjective assessments by trainer or managers, or by questionnaires or attitude scales (examples are given in Figure 8.7). One note of warning: adults, especially mature adults, are likely to be resistant to any suggestion of school and the classroom, and in the sensitive area of equal opportunities you may decide to settle for the less accurate approach of subjective appraisal.

**Figure 8.6** *Examples of knowledge tests*

*Short answer tests*

What is the difference between positive action and positive discrimination?

*True/false tests*

Positive action is unlawful        True/False

*Multiple choice tests*

In 1990, women's average gross hourly earnings as a percentage of men's were (please tick the correct answer):

65.9%      76.6%      89.3%      98%

*Essay-type questions*

Describe the difference between various types of questions and suggest how these may best be used when interviewing.

**Figure 8.7** *Examples of attitude measurement*

(Thurstone and Likert scales measure an individual's agreement or disagreement with a number of statements.)

*Example of Thurstone scale*

1. A degree of sexual and racial harassment is inevitable whenever you get groups of people working together.                                          Agree/Disagree
2. The only way a woman can get to the top is by behaving like a man. Agree/Disagree
3. It's not safe to employ anyone who has been in prison.            Agree/Disagree

*Example of Likert scale*

Tick one box only.

Women shouldn't expect to raise families and have successful careers

☐     strongly agree
☐     agree
☐     uncertain
☐     disagree
☐     strongly disagree

*Semantic differential scale*
(This consists of a statement followed by pairs of evaluative adjectives connected by either five or seven point scales. By comparing the learners' ratings made before and after the training, a measure of attitude change is obtained.)

Positive action training is (please tick)

divisive |___|___|___|___|___| cohesive

necessary |___|___|___|___|___| unnecessary

fair |___|___|___|___|___| unfair

discriminatory |___|___|___|___|___| non-discriminatory

## Contamination

Both validation and evaluation may be contaminated by external factors such as:

| *Validation* | *Evaluation* |
|---|---|
| domestic factors such as comfort of room, ease of access, etc. | rest of work team attitude of manager other reading |
| the rest of the group | other training |
| learning/teaching styles | change in work methods |
| individual's pre-course perceptions | pre-course perceptions |

The question to be borne in mind is, 'Would this have happened without the training?'

## Conclusion

If training is to be not only effective but seen to be effective and regarded as an integral part of the management process, it is necessary to have the means of determining

- whether the training activity met its objectives
- the longer-term effects on performance.

Many of us have limited resources which may restrict us to the first item. However, in a controversial area like equal opportunities, you are likely to have to justify the investment in training, and carrying out evaluation exercises from time to time will help you to do this. Find a friendly department and see if it can help you to find evidence to show that the training you have provided has been effective and beneficial to the organization as a whole.

# Appendix. Equal Opportunities Training: Approaches and Events

## 1. The University of Southampton: A Cascade Model of Awareness Training

The University adopted a full equal opportunities policy in 1988, which included the statement that, 'The University is committed to a programme of action to make the policy fully effective'. Training is fully integrated with this policy. A fully representative Equal Opportunities Committee was established, and at its inaugural meeting set up a Training Working Group, which was given a budget to work with. Policy coordinators were also appointed to implement policy and general awareness training across the University.

During its first year, the Training Working Group identified a set of priorities for training, including a programme of general awareness. Money was made available for the development of a flexible training package as this was thought to be the most economical way of introducing equal opportunities to some 3,500 employees.

The material was presented to the policy coordinators in order to educate them, provide a model of how the material could be used, and give feedback on the content and usefulness of the training materials. The coordinators, who would be training in pairs, were also offered practice sessions.

The training was supported by the senior management of the

University. The vice-chancellor wrote to heads of department and other budgetary groups asking them to encourage staff to attend and to give staff permission to attend during working time. In addition, the trainers who developed the material provided a seminar for heads of department.

The pack was designed to be flexible enough to acknowledge the needs of everyone working in the higher education sector. It has received the Lady Platt Award for equal opportunities training.

This training approach has had several positive outcomes, including an increase in participation in the recent staff audit, further work on policies and practices, and requests for specific training.

The advantages of the cascade model are thought to stem from the involvement of existing staff throughout the institution. It can be tailored to match the stage of equal opportunities implementation as well as the particular culture of the organization. It encourages the identification and involvement of change agents, and provides them with an effective and interactive role at the grass roots. It is also a cost-effective means of ensuring that the staff come to 'own' the policy and apply it in their own situation.

## 2. Equal Opportunities Training at the Ministry of Defence

In 1982 a programme of positive action training for women was developed by two enthusiastic women trainers in the training department in an attempt to redress the imbalance at middle and senior management levels; this programme continues to be very successful. Otherwise, reference was made to equal opportunities in existing management programmes.

Some two years ago the Cabinet Office developed the Programme of Action to ensure Equality of Opportunity in Employment for People of Ethnic Minority Origin. Each government department adopted this programme and interpreted its training requirements in its own way. The Ministry of Defence decided that it was impractical to consider race in isolation when discussing Equal Opportunities training as there would inevitably be some overlap into issues of gender or disability. A three and a half day-course was developed which examined issues of race, gender and disability, with the greatest proportion of time being spent on race. Initially intended for personnel managers, it is now likely to be extended to line managers.

The course is not designed to change peoples' attitudes but to raise their awareness of these attitudes and so enable them to operate more clearly – 'to stir them into thought'. Some values and beliefs are challenged, but in a non-threatening way.

The course is considered to be both popular and effective with a continuing demand for places. Individual members of staff volunteer to attend – there is no compulsion. Judi Garstang, the Training Adviser, who was responsible for setting up the course, feels that it is so successful because it followed on from the Programme of Action: 'once the policy was decided, it was quite straightforward'.

# 3. The Implementation of a Local Authority Equal Opportunities Programme

### The Importance of Training

The authority has always had an active training programme with in-house courses, sponsorship for professional qualifications, trainee and apprenticeship schemes, and specialist training for social workers, housing and recreation workers. The introduction of an equal opportunities in employment policy in 1983 led to an increase in this provision.

At the introduction of the policy, the authority set up an Equal Opportunities Unit (four people) to implement the policy (backed by an Equal Opportunities Committee) and the training section was increased to nine people by 1986.

The importance of training was emphasized in order to:

- Generate new procedures effectively
- Challenge discrimination and prejudice
- Offer development opportunities to disadvantaged groups
- Reach recruitment, promotion and training targets for disadvantaged groups.

### Formulation

The training was entirely policy-driven in its initial stages. The policy focused on the recruitment process and this was the first area of training to be introduced. A three-day course was designed with the help of an external consultant. All members of staff due to interview were required to attend. The courses ran every week initially and then every fortnight for two years.

The programme of in-house courses continued (management, communication skills, etc.) but case studies and other material were re-written to be gender-free and to raise issues of equal opportunities in each course. Notes of guidance on the conduct of training courses, use of language, etc., were prepared for all the external trainers used on in-house courses.

The process continued with a one-day seminar for heads of departments on a strategy for the promotion of equal opportunities in their departments. By this stage, monitoring information was available on all current staff and heads of department were asked to use this to prepare action plans and propose targets. This included departments setting targets for access to sponsorship for qualification courses and for gender and race targets for traineeships and apprentices. These plans were presented to the Equal Opportunities Committee and progress reviewed each year.

The next area was a one-day equal opportunities action planning seminar for managers of local services. These were conducted area by area and concentrated on their role in developing equal opportunities in employment and in the service they were in charge of. This was the first training for which a training needs analysis was undertaken. It was conducted by observation and interview with the managers and a sample of their staff.

While this process of implementation-related seminars continued, a number of specialized courses were set up. These included:

Assertion for women staff
Career development workshops
Interviewee skills.

All were intended to build confidence and skills.

A number of courses on specific areas of the policy were then established:

Anti-racism workshops (for heads of department initially and then for other managers)
Disability management
Challenging heterosexism
Men and women working together.

Apart from the anti-racism workshops, attendance on these courses was voluntary. This resulted, to some extent, in failing to reach those most in need of them.

## Training Policy

The training provided was determined by the development and implementation of the equal opportunities policy and by the action plans developed by departments, based on monitoring information. No training needs survey was undertaken, although the content of each course was based on observation and interview.

The training on implementation issues was undertaken by internal training staff, initially assisted by external consultants. The specialized courses were run by external consultants. The Equal Opportunities Unit was involved in planning the programme and members of the Unit contributed to some of the courses.

## Examples of Training Events

---

**INTRODUCTION TO ASSERTIVENESS SKILLS; A WORKSHOP FOR WOMEN ACADEMIC STAFF**

*Timing:* Two half-days

*Objectives:* To give an introduction to assertiveness theory, and to practise some of the techniques described. Particular attention will be paid to the needs of women staff.

*Outline programme:* The workshop consists of two half-days, giving the opportunity between sessions to reflect and to try out some new approaches discussed in the workshop. You will be expected to attend both days. The workshop will be highly participative, and will include some theory, discussion and plenty of opportunity for practical application of techniques and strategies.

A questionnaire will be sent to you two weeks before the workshop for you to test how assertive you are. It is for your own personal use, but you may like to bring it with you for general discussion.

*Day 1*
- Introductions
- Objectives (including gender issues)
- Definition
- Modes of behaviour
- Self-confidence and self-esteem
- Human rights
- Body language
- Listening skills
- Questionnaire to identify own areas of training need
- Preparation for day 2

*Day 2*
- Review of day 1
- Saying no – role plays and video extracts
- Oral strategies
- Role play
- Internal dialogues
- Negative thinking
- Modes of behaviour
  - boundaries
  - effects on people
- Coping with criticism
- Meetings
- Action plans
- Course evaluation

(University College London)

---

ONE-DAY SELECTION SKILLS COURSE

9.00   Introductions

9.15   Résumé of Sex Discrimination, Race Relations and Disabled Persons Acts
*direct and indirect discrimination; positive discrimination and positive action;
GOQs; quotas and targets*

9.30   Removing barriers
*small groups identify procedures, practices or policy which could lead to unfair selection
in the following stages of recruitment (each group looks at three items):*
   *the vacancy – job descriptions and person specifications*
   *the method of publicizing the vacancy*
   *the advertisement*
   *application forms*
   *aptitude tests*
   *short-listing*
   *composition of panel/type of interview*
   *conduct of interview*
   *assessment of candidates*
   *medical information*
   *references*

10.00   Full Group Review
*To establish a logical recruitment process and good practice at each stage*

10.45   Coffee

11.00   Job descriptions and person specifications
*Tutor input on functions and style, including potentially discriminatory features*

11.15   Designing a person specification
*Small groups design a person specification based on a job description, following the
tutor's pro-forma*

11.45   Full group review
*Person specifications compared and discussed. Six of the 'best' items selected to form a
person specification to be used by groups in their practice interviews*

12.15   Structuring the interview
*Tutor input and handout on the purpose of the interview and the structure and roles
within it. Full group discussion on main interview 'faults', eg, halo and horns*

12.45   Lunch

1.45   Interview skills
*Questioning: exercise to identify question types followed by a description of the 'funnel'
approach to probing for information. Handout.*
*Listening and note-taking: exercise in listening to a taped interview and taking notes
from it. Handout.*

2.20 Preparation for practice interviews
*Small groups given the application forms for two 'volunteer' interviewees. Structure and prepare to interview using the person specifications prepared in the morning*

3.00 Practice interviews
*Each of four groups interviews one candidate and observes the other candidate being interviewed. Tutor observation and feedback.*

4.15 Making the assessment
*Each group rates each candidate on an assessment form based on the match to each item on the person specification: meets, fails to meet, unknown*

4.35 Making the choice
*Each group presents evidence for their rating to the tutors. Stereotyping, prejudice or discrimination discussed during the process*

5.15 Questions and review

(City University, London)

---

## LUNCHTIME AWARENESS SEMINAR ON EQUAL OPPORTUNITIES

12.00 Introductions

12.10 What is equal opportunities?
*Brief lecture and handouts on the history of equal opportunities and the main UK legislation*

12.30 Equal opportunities terms
*Question and answer session on the meaning of direct and indirect discrimination, positive action and positive discrimination, prejudice and stereotyping, quotas, targets and GOQs*

12.50 Why have a policy?
*Brainstorming and discussions about the need for a policy – the reasons and benefits for the organization – maximizing support*

1.15 Discrimination and prejudice
*Small group discussion on the impact of both in an organization and how to tackle them; ways of challenging stereotypes; barriers to progress*

1.40 Language and images
*Large group discussion on producing a positive image of the organization*

2.00 Planning a follow-up and close

(City University, London)

# Bibliography

We give below a list of some books, videos and training material which you may find useful; references found in various chapters have also been included. We have limited the list to material which is well known and easy to obtain, but this does not mean that we have evaluated it or are recommending its use.

## Books

Commission for Racial Equality (1991) *Code of Practice for the Elimination of Racial Discrimination and the Promotion of Equality in Opportunity in Employment,* London: CRE.

Employment Service (1990) *Code of Good Practice on the Employment of Disabled People,* London: ED.

Equal Opportunities Commission (1992) *Code of Practice for the Elimination of Discrimination on the Grounds of Sex and Marriage and Promotion of Equality of Opportunity in Employment,* Manchester: EOC.

Income Data Services Ltd (1984) *'Sex Discrimination and Equal Pay,* Employment Law Handbook 29, London: IDS.

Income Data Services Ltd (1990) *Race Discrimination,* Employment Law Handbook 48, London: IDS.

Institute of Personnel Management (1988) *Equal Opportunities Code,* London: IPM.

Lewis, V and Habeshaw, S (1990) *53 Interesting Ways to Promote Equal Opportunities in Education,* Technical & Education Services Ltd.

Straw, J (1990) *Equal Opportunities – the way ahead,* London: Institute of Personnel Management.

Walton, F (ed.) (1986) *Encyclopaedia of Employment Law and Practice,* Professional Publishing Ltd.

# Videos

'It Worked Fine', Disablement Advisory Service (free).

'It Can Be Done', Disablement Advisory Service (free).

'Let's Be Fair', Mast Learning Systems for the Cabinet Office (available from CSL Vision, PO Box 35, Wetherby, West Yorkshire LS23 7EX; tel. 0937 541010).

'A Tale of O', Melrose Film Productions Ltd.

# Training Packs

'Be Fair', British Association for Commercial and Industrial Education (1987).

'Equal Opportunities in Practice', CVCP Universities' Staff Development Unit (1992).

'Equal Opportunities Learning Programme', The Cabinet Office (1992).

'Managing Diversity', The Cabinet Office (1991).

# Organizations

The following organizations are a useful source of booklets and other information:

Commission for Racial Equality, Elliot House, 10-12 Allington Street, London SW1E 5EF (071-828 7022).

Employers' Forum on Disability, 5 Cleveland Place, London SW1Y 6RL (071-321 6591).

Equal Opportunities Commission, Overseas House, Quay Street, Manchester M3 3HN (061-833 9244).

Institute of Personnel Management, IPM House, Camp Road, London SW19 4UX (081-946 9100).

Trades Union Congress, Congress House, Great Russell Street, London WC1B 3LS (071-636 4030).

# References

Alderfer, C P (1972) *Existence, Relatedness and Growth: Human needs in organisational settings*, New York: Free Press (London: Collier-Macmillan).

Commission for Racial Equality (1989) *Training: The Implementation of Equal Opportunities at Work Volume 1*, 2nd ed, London: CRE.

Daedal Training Ltd (undated) *Secretarial Development Manual*, Orpington, Kent: DTL.

Herzberg, F (1968) *Work and the Nature of Man*, London: Staples Press.

Hook, C (1990) 'Consultant's corner', *Transition*, February.

Kakabadse, A, Ludlow, R and Vinnicombe, S (1988) *Working in Organizations*, Harmondsworth: Penguin.

Laird, D (1978) *Approaches to Training and Development*, Wokingham: Addison-Wesley.

Local Government Training Board (1984) *The Trainer's Programme Unit 2: What do trainers do?*, London: Local Government Training Board.

Maslow, A (1954) *Motivation and Personality*, London: Harper & Row.

Tannenbaum, R and Schmidt, W (1958) 'How to Choose a Leadership Pattern', *Harvard Business Review*, March–April.

# Index